80 Morning Meeting IDEAS

for Grades K-2

Susan Lattanzi Roser

All net proceeds from the sale of this book support the work of Center for Responsive Schools, Inc., a not-for-profit educational organization and the developer of the *Responsive Classroom*® approach to teaching.

ISBN: 978-1-892989-47-5
Library of Congress Control Number: 2011942051

Cover and book design by Helen Merena

Center for Responsive Schools, Inc.
85 Avenue A, P.O. Box 718
Turners Falls, MA 01376-0718

800-360-6332
www.responsiveclassroom.org

Ninth printing 2018

Printed on recycled paper

Getting Each Day Off to a Great Start

Responsive Classroom® Morning Meeting is a fun, friendly, and powerful way to get each day off to a great start. These 20- to 30-minute daily whole-group gatherings help create community and reinforce academic and social skills in lively ways.

This book gives you 80 ideas and many tips to help you plan engaging and purposeful Morning Meetings for your class. These 80 ideas cover the four sequential components of Morning Meetings:

1 **Greeting** * Each child is greeted by name, the most basic way of providing a sense of belonging.

2 **Sharing** * Children share news or information about themselves, which helps them get to know one another and strengthen communication skills.

3 **Group Activity** * A whole-group activity reinforces learning and encourages cooperation and inclusion.

4 **Morning Message** * A brief note from the teacher to the class further reinforces skills and sparks children's excitement about what they'll be learning that day.

In these pages, you'll find ideas for 20 greetings, 20 sharings, 20 group activities, and 20 morning messages. Each idea comes with clear, step-by-step directions, along with tips for helping children succeed and for maximizing social and academic learning.

How to Use This Book

For practical tips and help in "mixing and matching" ideas based on children's academic and social needs and abilities, use the:

* **Ideas at a Glance** (pages 8–15)

* **Sample Combinations** (pages 199–201) of greeting, sharing, group activity, and morning message ideas

* **Morning Meeting Planners** (pages 202–203)

Also see "Teacher Language That Enriches Morning Meeting" on pages 204–205. You'll find sample reinforcing language and open-ended questions that allow children to benefit from the full power of the ideas in this book.

To see video clips of Morning Meeting in action in real classrooms, visit youtube.com/user/responsiveclassroom.

Take advantage of the mixture of routine and surprise, comfort and challenge, in this collection of ideas to plan Morning Meetings for your class all year long!

NOTE: This book is not intended to provide comprehensive instruction on *Responsive Classroom*® Morning Meeting. For that, refer to *The Morning Meeting Book*, 3rd edition, by Roxann Kriete and Carol Davis (Center for Responsive Schools, 2014) and the other resources listed on pages 206–207.

Three Keys to Planning Successful Morning Meetings

1. **Determine how much time you have and choose ideas accordingly.** Some of the ideas in this book may be easier to extend or shorten for your class than others.

2. **Consider students' learning objectives for the day.** Look for greeting, sharing, group activity, and morning message ideas that especially support or can be easily adapted to support these objectives.

3. **Think about students' strengths and challenges.** Where are they in their development? What are some recent challenges that they would benefit from working on? What social or academic skills might need a little extra reinforcement and practice?

Here's an example:

Second grade teacher Mr. Johnson observed that conflicts were increasing at recess and lunch. He decided to focus on team-building in the next Morning Meeting, so he chose the:

* Ball Roll greeting (page 32)

* Fun Food Finds sharing (page 82)

* Mouse Trap group activity (page 128)

* Let's Exercise morning message (page 166)

Scaffolding for Success

Just as for academic subjects, it's essential to break down Morning Meeting skills and routines based on students' developmental needs and abilities and then gradually put the pieces together. With some scaffolding, all the ideas in this book can work for any K–2 classroom. Use the following guidelines to help you adjust the complexity of an idea so that it's appropriate for students at any given point in the school year.

* **Phase in Morning Meeting** by teaching one component at a time. (The best order of introduction is greeting, group activity, morning message, and sharing, even though this isn't their eventual order in a full Morning Meeting.)

* **Break down routines into bite-size pieces.** For example, before introducing a greeting that involves saying a classmate's name, asking and answering a question, and doing a handshake, be sure you've taught—and students have a solid command of— each of these elements.

* **Use Interactive Modeling** to teach Morning Meeting skills and routines. (To learn more about Interactive Modeling, visit www.responsiveclassroom.org.) It helps to model these signals, which are used often in Morning Meeting:

  • I'm ready (for example, put thumb up)

  • Turn up the volume/speak up (for example, cup hand by ear)

  • Signal for quiet attention (for example, using a chime or raising one hand)

* **Use reinforcing language and open-ended questions** to help children build and expand their skills. (See pages 204–205 for examples of teacher language you can use to enrich Morning Meeting.)

* **Know that it's OK to repeat an idea multiple times.** Then, as children gain expertise, introduce variations one at a time. Students, especially young ones, like repetition.

* **Write out chants, songs, poems, and other helpful texts.** Also consider using anchor charts, such as number lines.

* **Keep it simple!** Doing so helps students stay focused and keeps them from getting overwhelmed.

You'll find specific scaffolding suggestions for greetings, sharings, group activities, and morning messages on pages 18, 62, 110, and 154.

Morning Meeting Supplies

Here are some supplies commonly needed for Morning Meetings:

* Ball of yarn
* Beach ball
* Beanbags
* Chart(s) of sentence starters and question starters (for sharings)
* Chime or other pleasant sound-maker

* Counting bears (or other counters)
* Easel chart and paper
* Flash cards
* Hand mirror
* Koosh ball
* Magnifying glass
* Markers

* Name cards (include photos if possible)
* Pair cards (same food, number, color, etc.)
* Playground ball
* Pointers
* Sticky notes (various sizes)

Some Suggestions

* **Keep supplies in one handy place**—a basket under the chart stand, for example.

* **Keep the Morning Meeting space clear**, so it's inviting and easy for children to gather in a circle. Post the Morning Meeting rules where they can be seen during the meeting.

* **Save each message**, song chart, and so on that you create for possible reuse. Consider displaying them at the end of the year so children can see all that they did during Morning Meeting!

When You Have a Guest (Substitute) Teacher

* **Plan a Morning Meeting that students will enjoy and can do smoothly.** You may want to create a standard Morning Meeting plan for all guest teacher days—for example:

  * We're So Glad You're Here Today greeting (page 28)

  * What's New? Chant sharing (page 72)

  * Jolly Jump Up group activity (page 114)

  * Guest Teacher morning message (page 180)

* **Provide the guest teacher with instructions for each Morning Meeting component.** You can use pages from this book for this purpose.

* **Prepare students in advance.** Ask an adult to role-play being a guest teacher with the class. Assign students to help with Morning Meeting tasks they have experience in doing, such as being the first ball-roller or guesser.

Greeting Ideas AT A GLANCE

TITLE	PAGE	CONTENT AREA	SKILLS REINFORCED*
Who Do You See?	20	Language Arts	Choral chanting, paying attention
We'll Cheer Hooray	22	Language Arts/Music	Focusing, voice volume
Stand and Reach Up High	24	Language Arts/Music	Singing/chanting, coordination
We're So Glad You Came to Play	26	Language Arts/Music	Reading fluency, timing, learning full names
We're So Glad You're Here Today	28	Language Arts/Music	Singing/chanting, creative thinking
Friends in Our Class	30	Language Arts/ Social Studies/Music	Keeping a steady beat, snapping fingers
Ball Roll	32	Phys Ed	Coordination, sequencing
Knock, Knock	34	Language Arts	Learning/using full names
Skip Two	36	Math	Counting, number relationships
Micro-Wave	38	Language Arts	Using clear voices, wordplay
Here We Are Together	40	Language Arts/Music	Singing/chanting in unison, learning names

TITLE	PAGE	CONTENT AREA	SKILLS REINFORCED*
Round the Circle	42	Math	Coordination, clockwise/counterclockwise directions
Chant Your Name	44	Language Arts	Keeping a steady beat, cooperation
Hand Stack	46	Math/Phys Ed	Coordination, cooperation
The Frog	48	Science/Language Arts	Coordination, creative thinking
Magnifying Glass	50	Science	Welcoming language, using a magnifying glass
The Roaring Greeting	52	Language Arts	Creative thinking, keeping a steady beat
TA DA!	54	Language Arts	Coordination, creative thinking, timing
Backward Day Handshake	56	Language Arts	Sentence structure, sequencing
Dove of Peace Handshake	58	Language Arts/Phys Ed	Coordination, left/right, sequencing

*The following skills apply to all of the greeting ideas listed above: self-control, friendly body language, listening, clear and audible speaking, assertiveness, and turn-taking.

Sharing Ideas AT A GLANCE

	TITLE	PAGE	CONTENT AREA	SKILLS REINFORCED*
Focused Topic Dialogue Sharing	**Family Photo**	88	Language Arts/Social Studies	Speaking clearly, using several complete sentences
	Name One Thing	90	Language Arts	Comprehension, recall
	Share Bear Jar	92	Language Arts	Topic sentence, supporting details, concluding statement
Open Topic Dialogue Sharing	**What Could We Share About?**	94	Language Arts	Brainstorming, decision-making, critical thinking
	Making Connections	96	All Subjects	Public speaking, making connections
	Asking Questions	98	All Subjects	Asking and responding to questions respectfully
	Mirror My Feelings	100	All Subjects	Expressing empathy
	Questions & Comments	102	All Subjects	Asking and responding to questions, making appropriate comments
	A Lesson on Sharing and Responding to Serious News	104	All Subjects	Expressing empathy

*The following skills apply to all of the sharing ideas listed above: self-control, friendly body language, listening, clear and audible speaking, assertiveness, turn-taking, decision-making, formulating questions, and understanding different points of view.**

Group Activity Ideas AT A GLANCE

TITLE	PAGE	CONTENT AREA	SKILLS REINFORCED*
A Counting Rhyme	112	Math/ Language Arts	1–1 correspondence, sequencing, numerical order, singing/chanting
Jolly Jump Up	114	All Subject Areas	Word, number, & shape recognition
Bug in the Rug	116	Science	Observing, memory skills, giving clear clues, chanting
Black Socks	118	Language Arts/Music	Focusing, singing as a group and in rounds, word recognition
Aka Baka Soda Cracker	120	Math/Phys Ed	Coordination, keeping a steady beat, predicting
Lost Tooth Poem	122	Language Arts/Health	Reading poetry, word recognition, rhyming, keeping a steady beat
Off My Back	124	All Subject Areas	Deduction, estimation
Apples, Peaches, Pears, and Plums	126	Language Arts/Social Studies/Science	Predicting, letter/word recognition, keeping a steady beat
Mouse Trap	128	Phys Ed	Coordination, focusing
Rumpelstiltskin	130	Language Arts	Decision-making, deduction
Purple Soup	132	Language Arts/Music	Pantomiming, teamwork, singing/chanting

TITLE	PAGE	CONTENT AREA	SKILLS REINFORCED*
Hello, Neighbor!	134	Language Arts/Music	Sequencing, left and right, synonyms, singing/chanting
Bluebird, Bluebird	136	Language Arts/ Science/Music	Following directions, coordination, observation, singing/chanting
The Teacher's Cat	138	Language Arts	Keeping a steady beat, adjectives, alphabetical order, creative thinking
Who Has Seen the Wind?	140	Language Arts/ Science	Sequencing, reading with expression, word recognition
Fruit Salad	142	All Subject Areas	Coordination, concept recognition
Herman the Squirmin' Worm	144	Language Arts/ Science/Music	Sequencing, pantomiming, size relationships, singing/chanting
Ahoy Matey!	146	Social Studies	Coordination, following directions, focusing, pantomiming
Super Gooney Bird	148	Language Arts/ Science/Music	Coordination, sequencing, memory, singing/chanting
The Swing— An Action Poem	150	Language Arts	Reading fluency, rhyming, 1–1 correspondence

*The following skills apply to all of the group activity ideas listed above: **self-control, friendly body language, listening, clear and audible speaking, assertiveness, turn-taking, predicting, analyzing, and problem-solving.**

Morning Message Ideas AT A GLANCE

Fluent Readers

TITLE	PAGE	CONTENT AREA	SKILLS REINFORCED*
Favorite Numbers	184	Math/Language Arts	Sequencing, computation skills
How's the Weather?	186	Science/Language Arts	Weather vocabulary, letter-sound recognition
Today Is a Special Day	188	Social Studies/Language Arts	Exploring historical facts and traditions
Count Your Name	190	Math/Language Arts	Counting, categorizing, odd/even
Where in the World?	192	Social Studies/Language Arts	Categorizing, geography
How Do We Do It?	194	Language Arts	Verbs and adverbs, creative writing, brainstorming
Searching the Solar System	196	Science/Language Arts	Organization, classification, compare and contrast

*The following skills apply to all of the morning message ideas listed above: self-control, friendly body language, listening, clear and audible speaking, assertiveness, turn-taking, reading fluency, decoding, and following directions.

Greetings

Each greeting idea in this book takes 2–6 minutes.

Goals of Greeting

* Set a positive tone for the day
* Help children learn each other's names and expand their range of friendships
* Give children a sense of recognition and belonging
* Help children practice offering hospitality

Greeting Skills to Model

Common skills that children need for success with greetings:

* Sitting/standing in the circle
* Speaking in a clear, friendly voice
* Singing/chanting loudly enough
* Using friendly body language
* Listening respectfully (facing the speaker, making eye contact, and so on)
* Choosing different classmates to greet each day (not just their best friends)
* Shaking hands (traditional, gentle fist bump, and so on)
* Waiting for a turn
* Signaling to show they've been greeted already

Reteach common greeting skills after breaks (long weekends, vacations) and whenever new students join the class.

17

Scaffolding Greetings

You can adjust the complexity of each greeting to better meet students' needs and abilities. For example:

* Use the Tips for Success to prepare students for each greeting. In general, start with simple greetings. Build on mastered skills when introducing new greetings.

* Teach and model the use of first names before moving on to full names.

* For greetings with multiple steps, do one step at a time. Add in subsequent steps one at a time.

* Reteach and remodel if children don't meet expectations for a step or routine.

* Once students learn basic greeting skills, use the Variations to add challenge and enrichment.

Younger children can also benefit from having seating spots marked on the rug to help them fit into the circle space evenly.

Ideas for Handshakes and Waves

Add variety and challenge by replacing the traditional hand-shake and wave with these alternatives:

* Micro-wave (wave a pinky)
* High five
* Double high five (use both hands)
* Fist bump
* Pat on the back
* Elbow rub

. . . .
A Musical Note:

Some greeting ideas in this book involve singing. You can search online to learn the tunes or simply do these greetings as chants.

Greetings in Various Languages

Saying "good morning," "hello," or a similar salutation in a language other than English enriches children's learning. Search online or ask native speakers of the language for help with pronunciations and proper usage.

* American Sign Language (to sign "hello," move hand out from the forehead, using a forward and downward movement, like a salute)

* Chinese (Mandarin)—Ni hao (nee **hah**-o)

* French—Bonjour (bon-**zhoor**)

* German—Guten Morgen (**goo**-ten **mor**-gen)

* Haitian Creole—Bonjou (**bon**-zhou)

* Hebrew—Shalom (shah-**lome**)

* Hindi—Namaste (nah-**mah**-stay)

* Hmong—Nyob zoo (nayaw jhung)

* Italian—Buon giorno (buon **jor**-no)

* Japanese—Ohayō (oh-hi-**oh**)

* Navajo—Yá'át'ééh abíní (**yah**-ah-tay ah-**bin**-ih)

* Portuguese—Bom dia (bon **dee**-a)

* Romanian—Buňa dimineata (**boo**-nuh dee-mee-**nyah**-tzuh)

* Russian—Dobroe utro (**da**-bray **oo**-tra)

* Spanish—Buenos días (bway-nos **dee**-ahs)

* Swahili—Jambo (**jahm**-bo)

* Vietnamese—Xin chao (seen chow)

Who Do You See?

How to do it:

GREETING

Skills
choral chanting,
paying attention

Materials
song chart
(optional)

1 Choose the first student to be greeted.

2 The group chants: *[Maria, Maria], who do you see?*

3 Maria turns to her neighbor, smiles, and responds: *I see [Johnny] looking at me!*

4 Johnny turns toward Maria and smiles back.

5 The group chants: *Johnny, Johnny, who do you see?*

6 Repeat Steps 3 through 5 around the circle until all have been greeted.

Tips for Success

* Model chanting and responding in time with the group (as their name is chanted, children look and smile at their neighbor, who turns and smiles back at them).

* Reinforce positive behaviors. For example: "You are all paying close attention."

. . . .

Variation

* Replace *who do you see* with *what do you hear*. For example, Johnny makes a sound, such as snapping fingers, and Maria says, "I hear Johnny snapping fingers next to me."

We'll Cheer Hooray

How to do it:

1 Display the words if needed:

> *[Child's name] came to school today.*
> *We're so glad, we'll cheer*
> *Hooray!*

2 Choose a child to be greeted first; as a class, sing the verse to him. On *Hooray!*, children raise their hands and chant the word with joy.

3 Repeat until all children have been greeted.

4 End the greeting song with this concluding verse:

> *We see good friends here today.*
> *We're so glad, we'll cheer*
> *Hooray!*

On this last *Hooray!*, children again raise their hands and chant with joy.

GREETING

Skills
focusing,
voice volume

Materials
song chart
(optional)

Tips for Success

✳ Teach the words and tune.

✳ Model safe cheering of *Hooray!* with raised hands, at an appropriate volume.

· · · · · · · · · · · · · · · · · ·

Variations

✳ Substitute other verbs for *cheer* (*whisper, sing, clap, snap,* and so on).

✳ Use sign language for parts of the song.

Stand and Reach Up High

How to do it:

1 Display the words if needed:

> *Stand up [Marta]. Stand up [Teddy].*
> *Stand up [Anna]. Stand up [Juan].*
> *Reach up very high now.*
> *Reach up to the sky now.*
> *Turn around. Now sit down.*

2 To the tune of "Frère Jacques," sing the words as a group, inserting the names of the first four children as you go in order around the circle.

3 As the children hear their names, they stand up and follow the song's directions.

4 Continue around the circle until all have been greeted.

Tips for Success

* Model how to carefully stand, reach up, turn, and sit down in your spot.

* Reinforce positive behaviors. For example: "I saw some fancy turns that were done carefully."

* Before using this greeting again, remind students: "What will we need to do to stay safe as we stand and turn?"

. . . .

Variations

* Randomly select children around the circle so they have to listen carefully for their name.

* Adapt other songs for this greeting, such as "Colors" by Hap Palmer.

We're So Glad You Came to Play

How to do it:

1 Display the words if needed (sing to the tune of "If You're Happy and You Know It"):

> *Good morning, [first name and last name].*
> *How are you? [clap, clap]*
> *Good morning, [repeat first and last name].*
> *How are you? [clap, clap]*
> *How are you this special day?*
> *We're so glad you came to play.*
> *Good morning, [repeat first and last name].*
> *How are you? [clap, clap]*

2 Pass out the name cards. Have children put the cards face down in front of them. Choose who will be greeted first.

3 Sing the song together, inserting the first child's name.

GREETING

Skills
reading fluency,
timing, learning
full names

Materials
name cards,
song chart
(optional)

4 When the first child hears her name, she holds up her name card(s) so all can see, and returns the card(s) to the floor after the clapping.

5 Repeat Steps 3 and 4 until all have been greeted.

Tips for Success

* Teach the words and tune. Practice the clapping before using names.

* Model when and how to hold up name cards. (Prepare name cards in advance, with each student's first and last names spelled out in clear, large letters.)

* To help with pronunciation, ask children to state their first and last names.

. . . .

Variation

* Instead of name cards, write the names on a chart. When you point to a name, that child stands up. Children remain standing until all have been greeted.

Another fun way to use "Frère Jacques" to learn names.

We're So Glad You're Here Today

How to do it:

GREETING

Skills
singing/chanting,
creative thinking

Materials
name cards,
song chart
(both optional)

1 Display the words if needed:

> *There is [Lisa].*
> *There is [Ricky].*
> *That's her name.*
> *That's his name.*
> *We're so glad you're here at*
> *We're so glad you're here at*
> *School today*
> *School today.*

2 Decide on a greeting order. For example, go around the circle or hold up name cards.

3 To the tune of "Frère Jacques," sing the words as a group.

4 As the children see or hear each name, they gesture in a friendly way to that classmate.

Tips for Success

✳ Model friendly gesturing.

✳ Before doing this greeting, briefly brain-storm with children how they could respond when the class sings their name. (Guide children toward ideas such as smiling, waving, and nodding.)

Variations

✳ Choose another simple folk song and adapt its words into a greeting.

✳ After the greeting, do a quick fist-to-five check to see how well children know one another's names: "Hold up a closed fist to show 'I don't know any classmate's name,' three fingers to show 'I know some names,' or five fingers to show 'I know everyone's name.'"

Friends in Our Class

Skills
keeping a
steady beat,
snapping
fingers

Materials
song chart
(optional)

How to do it:

1 Display the words if needed:

Refrain

Friends in our class [snap, snap],
Friends in our class [snap, snap],
Friends in our class, friends in our class,
Friends in our class [snap, snap],

There's [Robert] and there's [Lia],
There's [Wen] and there's [Ian],
There's [Tyler] and there's [Lebron],
We're here to learn and play!

2 As the class sings or chants together, insert the names of the first six children in order around the circle.

3 Students may do a friendly gesture as they hear their names.

4 Continue around the circle, repeating the refrain after greeting six children.

Tip for Success

＊ Teach the tune and words. Model snapping fingers to keep time and making friendly gestures (if used).

. . . .

Variations

＊ Substitute other actions for snapping (for example, hand clapping, knee slapping, foot stomping, or head nodding).

＊ Use sign language for words such as *learn* and *play*.

Ball Roll

Use a ball
to help build coordination
and cooperation.

GREETING

Skills
coordination,
sequencing

Materials
playground
ball (or similar
ball)

How to do it:

1 With everyone seated in the circle, choose the first greeter. She says a friendly "Good morning, [child's name]" to someone across from her.

2 The receiver greets her back in the same way.

3 The greeter gently rolls the ball to the receiver, who becomes the next greeter.

4 Continue until everyone has been the greeter and rolled the ball. (The first greeter will be the last receiver.)

Tips for Success

* Model when to greet and roll the ball, and careful ball rolling and catching. Also model what to do if the ball doesn't go where intended or is missed.

* Choose a simple way for students to show that they've been greeted (for example, arms folded or behind the back).

* Prompt students to remember expected behaviors. For example: "What's important for us to remember before doing this greeting?"

Variation

* Later in the year, challenge the class not to use any signal to show they've been greeted (so children can practice paying close attention to who needs to be greeted).

Knock, Knock

Use this old favorite to greet one another and learn last names.

How to do it:

1 Choose a student as first greeter.

2 The first greeter turns to the student on her left (the receiver), smiles, and pretends to knock on a door in front of the receiver:

> Greeter: *Knock, knock!*
> Receiver: *Who's there?*
> Greeter: *Maya* [greeter says own first name]
> Receiver: *Maya who?*
> Greeter: *Maya Gonzalez!* [greeter says own first and last name]
> Receiver and group chant:
> *Good morning, Maya Gonzalez!*

3 The receiver becomes the next greeter. Continue until everyone has had a turn as greeter.

GREETING

Skills
learning and using full names

Materials
none

34

Tips for Success

* Model knocking on the pretend door and showing a friendly face as greeter and receiver.

* Reinforce positive behaviors. For example: "That was so much fun! What did we do as a team that made this greeting work?"

. . . .

Variations

* Have the whole group act as the receiver. (The greeter knocks toward the middle of the circle.)

* Use a small cardboard " door" or empty picture frame for the greeter to hold and look through when stating her full name.

* Later in the year, assign partners and do this as a simultaneous partner greeting.

Skip Two

Skip counting is a fun way to use math for greetings.

GREETING

Skills
counting,
number
relationships
and sequencing

Materials
none

How to do it:

1 With everyone standing, begin the greeting by counting two people to your left.

2 Stand in front of the next person (the third person to your left) and say a friendly "Good morning, [Jose]." Jose returns the greeting.

3 Sit down in Jose's spot. Jose continues skip-counting in the same way.

4 As greeters continue around the circle, they count only those still standing.

5 The last person standing greets the whole class, who chorally greets her or him back. This last greeter takes your current spot; you return to your original spot.

Tips for Success

* Model friendly greeting and careful seat switching.

* Reinforce positive behaviors. For example: "You took care of classmates when they made a mistake. What a caring class we have!"

. . . .

Variation

* Have students choose the number to skip by. Write the number on the board or chart.

Micro-Wave

How to do it:

1 Choose a student as first greeter.

2 The greeter says a friendly "Good morning, [child's name]" to his neighbor, holds up one hand, and waves—using only his pinky finger.

3 Continue around the circle until everyone has been greeted.

Tips for Success

* Model a controlled pinky-finger wave.

* Before doing this greeting, consider connecting it to creative writing or other wordplays. For example: Display the word *microwave* and ask volunteers to explain this "play on words" (or teach that *micro* means "small or tiny").

* Reinforce positive behaviors. For example: "Your voices and waves looked and sounded so friendly!"

- -

Variations

* Create a "micro-shake" by interlocking pinky fingers and shaking hands when greeting one another.

* Brainstorm and then try some other wordplays for greetings, such as a "mega-shake" (shaking hands in an exaggerated way).

Here We Are Together

How to do it:

GREETING

Skills
singing/chanting in unison, learning names

Materials
song chart (optional)

1 Display the words if needed (sing to the tune of "Did You Ever See a Lassie?" or "The More We Get Together"):

> Here we are together,
> Together, together.
> Oh, here we are together,
> Back at school again.
> There's [Tia].   Hi, [Tia]!
> And [Sang].   Hi, [Sang]!
> And [Asa].   Hi, [Asa]!
> And [Katerina].   Hi, [Katerina]!
> Oh, here we are together,
> Back at school again!

2 Choose a place in the circle to start the greeting.

3 As a class, sing together and insert the names of the first four students in the circle.

4 As students sing a classmate's name, they make an exaggerated arch-like wave.

5 Continue around the circle in order, greeting four children at a time. End by singing just the last two lines (or "Oh, here we are together, All done with our greeting!").

Tips for Success

* Model safe and friendly large waving.

* The first few times you use this greeting, sing the name yourself ("There's Tia") and have the children repeat it along with the greeting ("Hi, Tia!").

* Reinforce positive behaviors. For example: "I noticed many of you paid close attention to everyone's names. Listening carefully helps us learn new things."

Round the Circle

It's fun to combine movement in opposite directions with a friendly "Hello."

GREETING

Skills
coordination, clockwise and counterclock-wise directions

Materials
none

How to do it:

1 As students stand in the circle, choose the first greeter.

2 The greeter walks clockwise around the inside of the circle and chooses a student by tapping him on the shoulder. She continues walking clockwise around the circle. The tapped student walks counterclockwise inside the circle.

3 When they meet, they stop, wave, and greet each other. The first greeter says, "Hello, [Vincent!]" The tapped student says, "Hello, [Isabella!]"

4 The tapped student is the next greeter. The first greeter sits down in his spot.

5 Continue until everyone has been greeted.

Tips for Success

* Model safe and careful moving inside the circle, gentle shoulder tapping, and stopping before greeting.

* Encourage children to choose a classmate whom they don't usually work or play with.

. . . .

Variations

* Once children master the greeting sequence, use hopping, skipping, tiptoeing, and so on. Model each movement.

* Invite children to use a variety of greetings (for example, a handshake, bow, or saying hello in a different language).

Chant Your Name

Children keep a steady beat as they chant and clap in unison.

GREETING

Skills
keeping a steady beat, cooperation

Materials
song chart (optional)

How to do it:

1 Display the refrain if needed:

> *Chant your name,*
> *And when you do,*
> *We will chant it back to you!*

2 Choose a place in the circle to start the greeting.

3 Students clap on knees and chant the refrain together.

4 From the starting place in the circle, the first four children take turns chanting their name alone. The class echoes each name while keeping a steady beat:

Child 1: *[Deborah]* Group: *[Deborah!]*
Child 2: *[Nicola]* Group: *[Nicola!]*
Child 3: *[Angelo]* Group: *[Angelo!]*
Child 4: *[Marcus]* Group: *[Marcus!]*

5 After four children chant, repeat the refrain. Continue around the circle in order until all have been greeted.

Tips for Success

✳ Model chanting at an appropriate volume, knee clapping, and keeping a steady beat.

✳ Reinforce positive behaviors by prompting students. For example: "What might be tricky about keeping a steady beat as a group? What could we do if we start clapping too fast?"

. . . .

Variation

✳ Invite creativity by replacing *chant* with other words (*sing, whisper, growl,* and so on).

Hand Stack

How to do it:

GREETING

Skills
coordination, cooperation

Materials
none

1 Choose the first greeter. She faces her neighbor and puts her hand out in front (palm down).

2 The neighbor puts his hand on top of hers; she places her free hand on top of his; and so on, until their hands are stacked above eye level and make an arch.

3 The greeter peeks under the arch and says, "Good morning, [Freddie]." The neighbor greets her back: "Good morning, [Jada]."

4 Freddie now turns to his neighbor. They begin stacking hands.

5 Continue until everyone has been greeted.

Tips for Success

* Model safe hand stacking and making eye contact while peeking under arched hands.

* Reinforce positive behaviors. For example: "I see students really peeking carefully and making eye contact before they say 'Good morning.'"

Variations

* For the greeting, playfully say, "Peek-A-Boo! I see you, [child's name]. Good morning!"

* If time is short, do as a simultaneous partner greeting.

The Frog

How to do it:

1 Assign partners around the circle and choose a student as first "frog."

2 Children squat low like frogs and face their partner.

3 The first "frog" jumps up, claps, and greets his partner: "Ribbit! Good morning, [Sofia!]"

4 The partner jumps up and returns the same greeting: "Ribbit! Good morning, [Luis!]"

5 The next pair greets each other and so on, until everyone has been greeted.

GREETING

Skills
coordination, creative thinking

Materials

Tips for Success

* Model how to safely squat, jump up, and clap.

* Reinforce learning connections. For example: "There are many ways to be creative with our voices. Being creative is what writers, artists, scientists, and many others do to come up with new ideas."

Variations

* Adapt the greeting to fit the day's events or season. For example: "Ribbit! Spring has sprung and so have we! Hi, Sofia!"

* As a class, brainstorm other frog sounds instead of *ribbit*. Do the same for other animals and motions. For example: "What other animals make distinctive sounds? How could we use those sounds in a greeting? What motions could we do?"

Magnifying Glass

A fun greeting that helps children get familiar with a science tool.

GREETING

Skills
welcoming language, using a magnifying glass

Materials
magnifying glass

How to do it:

1 Choose a student as first greeter. She says a friendly "Good morning, [child's name]" to her neighbor.

2 The greeter holds up the magnifying glass near her neighbor's face. She looks through it and says, "It's so nice to see you!"

3 The greeter carefully passes the magnifying glass to her neighbor.

4 The greeting continues around the circle.

Tips for Success

✳ Model looking at someone's face with a magnifying glass in a careful and respect-ful way, and how to pass the magnifying glass safely.

✳ At some point before doing this greeting, you may want to discuss personal space: "When is it OK to get really close to someone? When might it not be?" and "What could we say if someone gets too close for our comfort?"

- -

Variation

✳ Instead of a magnifying glass, students use their hands to make pretend binoculars.

The Roaring Greeting

Keeping a steady beat while roaring like lions makes for an exciting greeting!

GREETING

Skills
keeping a steady beat, creative thinking

Materials
song chart (optional)

How to do it:

1 Display the refrain if needed (accented sounds are in bold):

> Good **morn**ing, good **morn**ing,
> **Hear** us all **roar**ing!

2 Choose a starting place in the circle.

3 Children clap hands on knees and keep a steady beat as they chant together, inserting the names of the first four children in order around the circle:

> Good **morn**ing, [Ava!]
> Good **morn**ing, [Ben!]
> Good **morn**ing, [Kahil!]
> Good **morn**ing, [Camila!]

After each name is chanted, everyone roars like a lion and shows their "claws."

4 After four children have been greeted, repeat the refrain and greet four more. Continue until all have been greeted.

Tips for Success

* Model appropriate roaring and clapping with a steady beat.

* Reinforce positive behaviors. For example: "I heard appropriate levels of roaring. You remembered to take care of your own voices and your neighbors' eardrums."

* * * * * * * * * * * * * * * * * * * *

Variation

* Adapt the refrain: *snoring* (make a snoring sound at Step 3); *storming* (pound fists on floor); *scoring* (turn to neighbor and give a high five), and so on.

TA DA!

GREETING

Skills
coordination,
creative thinking,
timing

Materials
none

How to do it:

1 As children stand in the circle, name the first greeter.

2 The first greeter chooses someone across the circle to greet (the receiver).

3 The greeter extends one arm toward the receiver and says, "Heeeeere's [Anthony]!"

4 The people to the immediate left and right of the receiver respond "Anthony! TA DA!" while making a "TA DA" action.

5 The receiver, Anthony, becomes the next greeter. Continue until everyone has been greeted.

Tips for Success

* Model and practice choosing and doing a safe "TA DA" action (such as opening arms up wide) and using an appropriate voice level.

* Choose a signal to show who's been greeted (such as arms folded), or challenge students to remember who's been greeted.

* *

Variations

* Give the audience the option to clap or cheer after the "TA DA" action at Step 4.

* Give the receiver the option to bow or nod at Step 4.

Backward Day Handshake

How to do it:

1 Choose a student to begin the greeting.

2 The first greeter shakes hands with the person to her left and says, "[Alexis], morning good!"

3 The receiver responds, "[Gabriella], morning good!"

4 Continue around the circle until all have been greeted.

Tip for Success

* Model friendly handshaking and saying a backward greeting. Display a chart with backward greetings for reference (for example, "Max, you to Tuesday happy!").

· · · · · · · · · · · · · · · · · · · ·

Variations

* Later, do other Morning Meeting components backward. For example, read the message backward or sing a song backward. (Model and practice beforehand.)

* Shake hands with hands behind back and try to maintain eye contact.

Dove of Peace Handshake

How to do it:

1 Assign students partners in the circle and choose a student as first greeter.

2 The first greeter turns to her partner and holds her right hand up. The receiver holds his right hand up the same way. The two partners interlock thumbs and wave their fingers toward each other.

3 The greeter says, "Good morning, [Carlos]!" The receiver says, "Good morning, [Mia]!" Both keep waving.

4 Together, they end their greeting, saying "Let's have a peaceful day!" They raise their hands together and wave, as if a dove is flying away.

5 Continue the partner greetings around the circle.

Tips for Success

* In advance, model with a student how to hold right thumbs up to make half the dove (extend thumb from fingers; hold fingers straight up, no spaces in between them) and then interlock thumbs. Also model closed-finger waves, and the sequence of greetings and motions.

* Guide children toward positive behaviors by asking questions, such as "What might be challenging about doing this handshake? What can we do to make this work well?" and "When else might a peaceful greeting be used?"

*Sharings

Each sharing idea in this book takes 3–7 minutes.

Goals of Sharing

* Develop children's skills of caring and assertive communication
* Help children know one another
* Encourage habits of inquiry
* Provide practice in public speaking
* Strengthen language arts and other content area skills

Sharing Skills to Model

Common skills that children need for success with sharing:

* Deciding what to share
* Giving the thumbs-up "I'm ready to share" signal
* Using other signals such as "Me, too!" (page 75) and "Oh, that's new!" (page 77)
* Keeping sharing brief and focused
* Using a clear voice and an appropriate volume

* Listening and showing friendly, respectful body language
* Talking briefly and then letting the other person talk (for partner sharing)
* Responding to sharers with appropriate questions and comments
* Using complete sentences

Reteach common sharing skills after breaks (long weekends, vacations) and whenever new students join the class.

61

Scaffolding Sharings

In the twenty ideas on the following pages, you'll find:

* Three main sharing structures (around-the-circle sharing, partner sharing, and dialogue sharing)

* Focused topic dialogue sharing (you name the sharing topic) and open topic dialogue sharing (children choose the topic)

* Varying levels of responses expected from classmates after listening to sharers

Around-the-circle sharings are usually easiest. Dialogue sharings are the most challenging. Focused topics are usually easier than open topics.

The twenty ideas are presented in order from the generally least challenging to the most challenging. If your class is new to Morning Meeting sharing, you may want to try these twenty ideas in order. (Before using a new sharing idea, children should feel confident in doing the prior ones.) You may still want to go back to the easier ideas from time to time—to reinforce skills or just for fun.

For dialogue sharing, keep track of who shares. Avoid trying to squeeze in extra sharers because of holidays or other time crunches.

Sharing Topics

Choose inclusive topics that will enable all students to take part in the sharing comfortably. (You may want to list these and display them.) Avoid topics that could highlight differences in family economics or make some children feel excluded. Topics that are likely to be inclusive for all:

* Favorite foods

* Favorite games

* Favorite seasons

* Pets or animals

* A story or character you like

* A number you like

* A book you just read or heard read aloud

* Weekend activities

* A place you like or want to visit

* What's new in your life

* Family members and their ages

* Something you're good at

* A piece of schoolwork you're proud of

A Note About Sharing Objects

Also think about inclusiveness if you have students share about objects. For example, having children share about a piece of class work they did will be more inclusive than having them bring a favorite toy from home (since families have differing abilities to buy toys).

Ideal for when
school starts or
a new student joins
the class.

Apples or Bananas?

How to do it:

Around-the-Circle
SHARING

Skills
turn-taking,
decision-making,
using a clear
voice

Materials
none

1 Name two choices of fruit (for example, apple and banana). Tell the class everyone will get to say which choice they like better.

2 Give children time to think. Tell them to show a thumbs-up when they're ready.

3 Go around the circle. Each child gives a one-word response ("apple" or "banana") or says "No, thank you" if they don't like either choice.

Tips for Success

* Model the thumbs-up "I'm ready" signal and key sharing skills (short, clear responses; waiting patiently for your turn; listening quietly and showing friendly body language).

* Reinforce positive behaviors. For example: "You're remembering to use your 'loud and proud' voices" or "I noticed you all waited patiently for your turn to talk."

* To extend the learning after this sharing, ask reflective questions, such as "What did you notice about the kind of fruit we like?"

Variations

* Name two games, two animals, or two story characters for students to choose from.

* Increase choices to three. Once students are successful, guide them to come up with their own favorite choices in a category you name (see "My Favorite Game" on the next page).

My Favorite Game

Around-the-Circle
SHARING

Skills
reflecting
on personal
experiences,
decision-making,
using complete
sentences

Materials
none

How to do it:

1 Tell children to think of a favorite game and to be ready to tell the class. Name some games students know to jog their memory.

2 Give think time. When children are ready, they show the thumbs-up sign.

3 Be the first sharer. Use a complete sentence: "A game I like is 'Jolly Jump Up.'"

4 Go around the circle. Each child shares, following your example of using a complete sentence and an appropriate voice volume.

5 As children share, list the games they name on a chart. Tally repeats. (You can also create a bar graph of the information.)

Morning
Meeting

Tips for Success

* The first few times the class does this sharing, do a "Think-Aloud" to teach how to make a decision. Point to your head and think out loud: "Well, I like 'Bug in the Rug' and 'Jolly Jump Up,' but I have to pick just one. That's hard! I think I'll say 'Jolly Jump Up' because I always like playing it."

* Give reminders and reinforcements of expected behaviors, such as "What can we do to be friendly and respectful when waiting for our turn?" and "You remembered to stay quiet when others were sharing."

* Show enthusiasm for children's sharing. For example: "I learned some new ideas from you for games we could play together!"

* *

Variation

* Instead of games, have children share a favorite animal, story, or letter, or something they're having fun learning.

My Favorite Season... and Here's Why!

Around-the-Circle
SHARING

Skills
reasoning,
decision-making,
using complete
sentences

Materials
none

How to do it:

1 Tell children they will be telling the class what their favorite season is and why. Then ask them to name the four seasons. Briefly discuss the characteristics of each and list them.

2 Give think time. When children are ready, they show the thumbs-up sign.

3 Be the first sharer. Use a complete sentence and keep your "why" brief. For example: "My favorite season is summer because I love to go outside when it's warm."

4 Go around the circle. Each child shares, following your example of using a complete sentence.

Tips for Success

* Do this sharing once students feel more confident speaking to a group.

* Help students with the "why" explanation. For example: "What might be challenging about explaining why you like a certain season? What can you do to help yourself do that well?"

. . . .

Variation

* Instead of favorites, focus on predictions or another skill. For example: "What do you think will happen to the caterpillar and why? Let's share our predictions."

Who Remembers?

Around-the-Circle
SHARING

Skills
reasoning, recall

Materials
none

How to do it:

1 Tell children they'll share what their favorite place is and why. Then they'll play a game called "Who Remembers?" so they'll need to listen carefully to classmates' sharings.

2 Brainstorm examples of favorite places with the class (their kitchen, a playground, a place they go with friends, and so on).

3 Give think time. When children are ready, they show the thumbs-up sign.

4 Be the first sharer. Use a complete sentence, and keep your "why" succinct. For example: "My favorite place is the park because I like to read there."

5 After all have shared, challenge the class with four or five "Who remembers?" questions. For example: "Who remembers whose favorite place is the zoo? Does anyone remember why that is her favorite place?"

Tips for Success

* When brainstorming, guide children in naming everyday places to keep the sharing from becoming competitive.

* After sharing, invite children to briefly tell their strategies for remembering what classmates said.

Variation

* When children gain confidence and skill with this sharing, invite a few students to come up with the "Who Remembers?" questions in Step 5.

What's New? Chant

Around-the-Circle
SHARING

Skills
keeping a
steady beat,
reflecting
on personal
experiences

Materials
song chart
(optional)

How to do it:

1 Teach children the chant on the opposite page.

2 Give children some time to think of a piece of news to share when their name is chanted. When they're ready, they show the thumbs-up sign.

3 Start the chant while alternating knee and hand claps. Stop clapping while each student is sharing. Repeat the refrain after every four students. If children have no news, they say, "Not much. What's new with you?"

4 Be the first sharer so you can model keeping the sharing very short. Then go around the circle.

Refrain

Sharing! Sharing!
Listening and caring!

Chant

What's new, [Pedro]?
Pedro: *I ate pizza!*

What's new, [Lina]?
Lina: *I had a recital!*

What's new, [Demetri]?
Demetri: *I went bike-riding!*

What's new, [Jessica]?
Jessica: *I played with my puppy!*

Repeat refrain

Tips for Success

* Before the sharing, give examples of "news." Include simple things (like having pizza with family) and big events (like winning a contest). Stress that any news, big or small, is important.

* After sharing, express enthusiasm. For example: "We did it! It's not easy to keep to a beat, but you kept your news short and that helped."

You Like That Animal? Me, Too!

Around-the-Circle
SHARING

Skills
communicating a personal connection

Materials
none

How to do it:

1   Tell children that they will each share about an animal they like. They may use two sentences at most. Share your own example: "I like dogs. My family has a dog named Sylvie."

2   Give think time. When children are ready, they show the thumbs-up sign.

3   Be the first sharer. Repeat your sharing. Then invite children who also like dogs to show a "Me, too!" signal.

4   Go around the circle. Each child shares and classmates make the "Me, too!" signal if they like the same animal.

Tips for Success

✳ Before sharing, model and practice the "Me, too!" signal (fold down the middle three fingers; move hand, with thumb and pinky extended, back and forth toward the sharer and yourself).

✳ Reassure children they'll have a chance to talk more with others who like the same animals as they do. Ask: "When would be a good time to talk more?" Examples might include recess and lunch.

Variation

✳ Use academic topics: "What did you find most interesting about the book we read yesterday?" or "What did you find most challenging about the math activity?"

Book Talk

How to do it:

Children acknowledge connections or new things they learn from a sharer.

Around-the-Circle
SHARING

Skills
signaling personal connections and new learning

Materials
none

1 Tell children they will each name a book they have read or want to read. They may use two sentences at most. Share your own example: "I just read the book *How I Became a Pirate*. I really liked all the action it had."

2 Give think time. When children are ready, they show the thumbs-up sign.

3 Be the first sharer. Repeat your sample sharing. Then invite students who have also read, want to read, or have heard of *How I Became a Pirate* to show the "Me, too!" signal.

4 If children have not heard of this book, they wait until the "Me, too!" signals have been given. Then they show the "Oh, that's new!" signal.

5 Go around the circle. Each child shares and classmates give the "Me, too!" or "Oh, that's new!" signal.

Tips for Success

* Before sharing, model and practice the "Me, too!" signal (page 75) and the "Oh, that's new!" signal (use the index finger to point to the head on "Oh" and then point outward on "That's new!").

* After sharing, reinforce enthusiasm for learning new things. For example: "It's fun to find out what books this class likes. I look forward to learning more about you."

* Reinforce use of these signals during learning, such as when students share their writing.

My Family

Sharing about a familiar topic helps children practice one-on-one conversational skills.

Partner
SHARING

Skills
taking turns
speaking and
listening,
staying
on topic

Materials
none

How to do it:

1 Invite children to pair up with their neighbor in the circle.

2 Partners take turns sharing the names of people in their families. (Help partners agree on who will go first, if needed.)

3 Reinforce positive speaking and listening behaviors: "I see caring listeners and clear speakers." Redirect if one child is taking up too much "air time" by talking for too long.

4 On your signal, children end their sharing.

Tips for Success

* Before sharing, model being brief and concise. For example: "My family is made up of my spouse, Ted, my daughter, Gina, and our cat, Flower." Also model listening with interest to your partner (looking at partner, keeping quiet, nodding).

* Prepare children for having simultaneous conversations. For example: "What might be tricky with everyone talking at the same time? What can we do with our voices to be helpful?"

Variation

* Do this sharing on days of excitement. For example, before a school vacation, have partners share what they plan to do; before a major school event, have partners talk about what they hope to see or do there.

More About My Family

How to do it:

1 Help children form pairs (if possible, pair them with someone other than their partner for the "My Family" sharing on page 78).

2 Have partners take turns sharing the names of people in their families.

3 After each child has shared, say "free chat" or "buzz." Children begin talking freely about their families with their partners.

4 Reinforce positive behaviors. For example: "I notice partners waiting patiently for their turn to talk." Redirect if a child is doing too much of the talking.

5 Signal children after one minute to end the partner chats.

Tips for Success

* Before sharing, model how to free chat with a volunteer. Be sure to include taking turns to speak, being brief when you speak, and waiting until your partner has finished before talking.

* Afterward, help students reflect on the sharing. For example: "What was challenging about free chatting? What was easy?"

Variations

* Once children gain more expertise with free chats, extend the time by thirty seconds, then an additional minute, and so on.

* Do multiple rounds of free chats with different partners: Children stand in two concentric circles (an inside circle facing an outside circle). On your signal, everyone moves one step to the right and talks to a new partner.

Fun Food Finds

Do we both like this food? Dislike it? Children have fun free chatting to find out!

Partner
SHARING

Skills
finding commonalities

Materials
matching pairs of food cards or food cards cut in half

How to do it:

1 Distribute a food card to each student.

2 Students walk around to find the classmate with the matching food card. Partners sit down next to each other in the circle.

3 Invite partners to find out two things they have in common about the food. When they've found two things, they show a thumbs-up.

4 Prompt children to share their findings with the class. For example: "Raise your hand if you both like the taste of your food." "Who had in common that they both dislike how their food tastes?"

Tips for Success

* Before sharing, model with a volunteer
  how to talk about a food to find a commonality. For example, model asking: "Do
  you like or dislike this food?" and "What
  do you like (or dislike) about this food?"

* After sharing, reflect briefly with students.
  For example: "Was it tricky to find out your
  commonalities?" or "What did we learn we have
  in common about certain foods?"

. . . .

Variation

* Use other cards for matching, such as book titles, movies,
  colors, animals, and so on.

Reporting Food Finds

After children free chat, they share their findings with the whole class.

How to do it:

Partner
SHARING

Skills
finding commonalities, public speaking

Materials
matching pairs of food cards or food cards cut in half

1 Distribute a food card to each student. (Give students a different card than they had for "Fun Food Finds" on page 82.)

2 Students walk around to find the classmate with the matching food card. Partners sit down next to each other in the circle.

3 Invite partners to find out two things they have in common about the food. Once they've found two things in common, partners plan how to report their commonalities to the whole group.

4 When partners are ready to share, they show a thumbs-up.

5 Ask for a volunteer pair to go first. Then go around the circle.

Tips for Success

✳ Before sharing, model with a volunteer how to report to the class so that each partner shares one commonality.

For example: "My partner is Emma. We have pumpkin. One thing we have in common is that we do not like pumpkin pie." Then Emma shares: "The second thing we have in common about pumpkin is that we both like pumpkin bread!"

✳ Reinforce listening skills. For example: "I noticed everyone giving their full attention to the speaker. That was careful listening!"

· ·

Variation

✳ Use cards that relate to academic learning, such as vocabulary words or math facts.

My Partner's Pride

A good way to reinforce the often-challenging skills of encouragement and empathy.

Partner
SHARING

Skills
self-reflection, summarizing

Materials
none

How to do it:

1 Help children form pairs.

2 Tell them that they will take turns sharing about one thing they are proud of. Next, they will summarize what their partner told them and then share that with the class.

3 Give children a few minutes to partner chat about their "prides" and to prepare a brief summary for the class.

4 Reinforce positive speaking and listening behaviors; redirect as needed. Tell students when to start preparing their summaries.

5 On your signal, students end their partner chats. Ask a volunteer pair to go first. Then continue around the circle.

Tips for Success

* In advance, discuss how to share what people are proud of about themselves in respectful and caring ways.

  For example, ask: "How can we share what we are proud of in ways that are respectful to everyone? What if your partner feels like he or she is not proud about anything?"

* Before sharing, model with a volunteer how to summarize a partner share. For example: "This is Giovanni. He is proud of being a good sport when he plays soccer."

Focused Topic Dialogue
SHARING

Skills
speaking clearly,
using several
complete
sentences

Materials
children's family
photos, marker,
chart paper,
"Show Shelf"

Family Photo

How to do it:

1 Name the sharers for the day—up to three or four children. (For the first few times, you go first.)

2 The first sharer holds up a family photo (or drawing) and says three sentences about it. For example: "This is a photo of my family. We were at the zoo. I took this photo with my uncle's camera."

3 Continue with the other sharers for the day.

4 After the last sharing, ask one or two reflective questions. For example: "What's one thing you learned from today's sharings?"

Tips for Success

✳ In advance, model the sharing. Be sure children notice that you hold the photo still, speak in a clear voice, and say three complete sentences about the photo. As children point out these skills, list them.

✳ Remind children of the sharer's and audience's jobs. (List these as you discuss them or use the list you made above.) Afterward, reinforce listening skills. For example: "You were really paying close attention."

✳ Designate a "Show Shelf" where sharers can put items for classmates to view (not touch) later.

· ·

Variations

✳ Include academic themes, such as an item from home that begins with the letter "B."

✳ Invite children to clap after a classmate shares (to put closure to the sharing and add movement for the audience).

Name One Thing

Students build community and practice careful listening.

Skills
comprehension, recall

Materials
sharing skills list from page 89 (optional)

How to do it:

1 Name the day's sharers (up to three or four children).

2 The first sharer holds up a family photo or drawing, says three sentences about it, and then asks: "Who can name one thing I said?" The sharer calls on up to three students to respond.

3 Redirect and remind as needed. For example: "Raise hands if you want to respond."

4 Continue with the remaining sharers.

Tips for Success

* Model this sharing in advance. Ask a volunteer to be the sharer while you role-play an audience member. When the student asks, "Who can name one thing I said?" do a Think-Aloud.

  For example: "Hmm. Ahmad showed us a picture of his family. I remember his sister's name—Jameela. So that's what I'll say." Be sure the class notices that you named only *one* thing.

* Remind the children to use listening skills and act kindly. For example: "What are some strategies listeners use to remember what someone shared about?" "What could we do as the sharer if a classmate makes a mistake? What would be friendly?"

* *

Variation

* Vary sharing topics (see page 63 for ideas).

Share Bear Jar

SHARING

Skills
topic sentence, supporting details, concluding statement

Materials
jar with lid, counting bears/other counters

How to do it:

1. Name today's sharers (up to three or four children).

2. Give the jar, lid, and counting bears to the first sharer. Spread out the bears in front of the first sharer: one green, three yellows, one red.

3. The sharer tells about something she likes to do on weekends, using a topic sentence, three supporting details, and a concluding statement. Each time the sharer says a sentence, she places a bear in the jar (green for the topic sentence, yellow for a supporting detail, red for the concluding statement).

4. Continue with the other sharers.

Tips for Success

✳ Introduce this sharing in advance. Consider doing so during writing workshop. Sample modeling script:

"On the weekends, I enjoy scrapbooking."
(Put the **green** bear in the jar.)

"I love to look through my photos and decide how to put them in my scrapbook."
(Put a **yellow** bear in the jar.)

"Then I find some stickers to go with my photos."
(Put a **yellow** bear in the jar.)

"Finally, I write a fun caption for each photo."
(Put a **yellow** bear in the jar.)

"I feel proud when I've completed a scrapbook page."
(Put the **red** bear in the jar.)

"I'm done." (Place lid on jar.)

✳ After modeling, help children focus on paragraph skills. Ask: "What was the topic sentence? What were the supporting details? What was the concluding sentence?"

✳ The first few times the class does this sharing, reinforce skills by asking students questions after each sharing.

Open Topic Dialogue
SHARING

Skills
brainstorming,
decision-making,
critical thinking

Materials
chart, marker

What Could We Share About?

How to do it:

1 Explain that in a few days you will "open up the floor" so students can share about anything they'd like, and that today everyone will help generate a list of appropriate topics to share about with the class.

2 Provide examples of appropriate topics (for example, family photos) or use the list on page 63.

3 Give think time. Prompt as needed. For example: "What might we think about when deciding what topics are appropriate for sharing?"

4 Go around the circle to give each child a turn to suggest one sharing topic.

5 Write children's ideas on a chart. When an idea is not appropriate for public sharing, gently interrupt the child and explain why. For example: "Anna, that sounds like private news. We'll come back to you later for another idea."

Tips for Success

∗ When giving examples of appropriate topics (Step 2), avoid topics that can create competition among classmates, such as new toys.

∗ Tell students that if they are not sure whether something is appropriate for sharing, they should talk with you before they share. (However, it's best if you check in with the day's sharers to be sure.)

∗ Teach students that certain family news should be kept private and not shared with the class.

∗ To teach children how to share and respond to serious news, see page 104.

Students share about an appropriate topic of their choice and listeners can signal a connection.

Making Connections

SHARING

Skills
public speaking, making connections

Materials
list of appropriate topic ideas

How to do it:

1 Name today's sharers (up to three or four).

2 The first sharer says four to six sentences on a topic of her choice.

3 After each sharer, classmates give the "Me, too!" signal if they have a connection to the sharer. If they do not, they wait and then give the "Oh, that's new!" signal.

4 Continue with the other sharers.

5 As time allows, ask a reflective question (see examples on page 205) and reinforce speaking and listening skills.

Tips for Success

* In advance, model choosing one idea from the class topic list (page 94) and sharing about it. Make sure students notice that you kept your sharing brief, stayed on topic, spoke clearly, and made eye contact with the audience.

* If needed, review the "Me, too!" signal (page 75) and the "Oh, that's new!" signal (page 77).

* Display and review the class topic list for reference. Remind the next day's sharers to think about what they want to say about the topic of their choice.

* Always check in with the day's sharers to determine if their topic is appropriate.

Variations

* Offer a choice of signals for connections, including letting those with no connection signal first.

* If time allows, have children partner chat about the day's sharings or remind them how they can talk about the topic with the sharer later.

Asking Questions

How to do it:

SHARING

Skills
asking and responding to questions in respectful ways

Materials
chart paper, marker

1 Name today's sharers (up to three or four). Check in with sharers about their topic.

2 After the first sharer talks about a topic of his choice, he says, "I'm ready for questions."

3 The sharer calls on a student, who asks one question. The sharer responds to the question in a complete sentence. Repeat this step two more times.

4 Continue with the other sharers.

5 As time allows after sharing, ask a reflective question (see examples on page 205) and reinforce speaking and listening skills.

Tips for Success

* In advance, tell students that they can ask questions after the person's sharing. Brainstorm "question words" and list them, or use the question starters on page 107. Discuss what makes an effective question (for example, it prompts more than a "yes" or "no" answer). Add sample questions and tips to the list.

* Model the sharing. Be sure students noticed that you used the statement, "I'm ready for questions," and responded in complete sentences.

* At first, limit each sharer to taking three questions. Then increase the number as time allows.

Variation

* Before listeners ask questions, have them use the "Me, too!" or "Oh, that's new!" signals (pages 75 and 77).

Open Topic Dialogue

SHARING

Skills
expressing empathy

Materials
sentence starter examples (page 107), hand mirror

Mirror My Feelings

How to do it:

1 Name today's sharers (up to three or four). Check in with sharers about their topic.

2 The first sharer tells about something she is happy or excited about.

3 When she finishes sharing, she holds up the mirror and says, "Mirror my feelings." Then she calls on a student, who offers one empathic comment. The sharer acknowledges the comment simply (with a nod, for example). Repeat this step. Later, let sharers take more comments as time allows.

4 Continue with the other sharers.

5 As time allows after sharing, ask a reflective question (see examples on page 205) and reinforce speaking and listening skills.

Tips for Success

* In advance, teach children to mirror others' feelings; spread this teaching over a few Morning Meetings. Choose brief greetings, activities, and messages on these days. Here's how you can do that teaching:

  - Introduce this sharing: "Now that we have lots of experience sharing, we're ready for a new listening game called 'Mirror My Feelings.'"

  - Display some sentence starters (see page 107). Read them together.

  - Model sharing about something positive in your life. Show feelings, smile, and use positive language.

  - Have children partner chat about what they noticed (your words, facial expression, and body language). Then hold up the mirror and say, "Mirror my feelings." Go around the circle and let each pair say one or two mirroring comments.

Questions & Comments

How to do it:

1 Name today's sharers (up to three or four). Check in with sharers about their topic.

2 The first sharer talks about a topic of his choice (see page 63 for a list of appropriate topics).

3 When the first sharer finishes, he says, "I'm ready for questions and comments."

4 The sharer calls on a student, who asks one question or makes one comment. The sharer responds to the question or expands on the comment. Repeat this step two more times. Later, let sharers take more questions and comments. Continue with the other sharers.

5 If time allows after sharing, ask a reflective question (see page 205) and reinforce speaking and listening skills. For example: "Remember to keep sharings brief, stay on topic, and speak in a clear voice."

Tips for Success

* Review what makes for effective questions and empathic comments (see page 107 for sentence and question starters).

* If needed, model this sharing format. Be sure students noticed how you responded (used a complete sentence when responding to questions, nodded after comments).

. . . .

Variations

* To strengthen skills in responding with empathy, challenge the group to come up with at least two comments before asking questions.

* Children can use this format when sharing finished or in-progress work.

A Lesson on Sharing and Responding to Serious News

**A pet is missing. A relative has died.
A parent will be away for awhile.**

Serious events are not uncommon in children's lives. As your class strengthens its sense of community, students may want to share such news during Morning Meeting. To ensure that these sharings are safe for everyone and add to children's feelings of community, it's important to teach the skills of responding to serious news. A key to this teaching is to be clear and matter-of-fact. Try to teach this lesson early on, before the first serious news sharing.

Introduce the topic

You might say, "We have gotten strong in our sharing skills. We have practiced speaking clearly and responding respectfully. We have listed appropriate topics to share. Sometimes, you might want to share things that are worrying you or making you sad. We call this 'serious news.'" Give some examples of serious news that children might share.

Tell children to *always* check with you if they want to share serious news

Some serious news, while important to the student, may be news that the student should keep private. Some serious news may be too disturbing for the class to hear without special supports. Let students know that on open-topic sharing days, they should check with you first if they want to share some serious news. Explain why: "Sometimes, serious news needs to stay private. I will help you decide whether your news is appropriate for our class to hear." As an extra safety step, check in with all sharers yourself even if they don't come to you proactively.

Let students know they can always share any serious news with you in private.

Sometimes, even with these steps, a student may start to share private news. If so, gently interrupt, reiterate the guidelines for sharing private news, and redirect the student to talk with you later in the day after Morning Meeting. For example: "Teddy, it sounds like you have some private news. Let's meet during snack time and you can share it with me then. Is there something else you'd like to share with the class now that is appropriate for our Morning Meeting?"

Practice making empathic comments

Teach students that when a classmate shares serious news, their job is to notice how the sharer is feeling and show that they understand. Tell students that this is called showing empathy. "Let's practice," you might say. "Let's pretend I have some serious news about my kitten. As I share this news, pay attention to my words, facial expression, and body language so you can tell how I'm feeling." (You may also want to reteach "Mirror My Feelings" on page 100.)

* Say to the class, "My kitten is getting sick a lot and the vet doesn't know why. My kitten doesn't like to play or eat anymore. It's scary." Use facial expressions and body language that show you're scared and sad.

* Ask the class, "How do you think I'm feeling? Is there a sentence starter [see page 107] that you could use to mirror my feelings so I know you understand how I feel?"

* If needed, prompt students to name responses such as "You sound sad" and "I'm sorry to hear that." Simple, caring responses are best.

* Help the class avoid denial-of-feelings statements such as "Oh, it's no big deal. He'll be fine. You're worrying too much." Also, remind the class to avoid making responses that are about themselves and take the focus off the sharer. Talk about why these would not be helpful—people tend to feel better if we let them know that we understand their feelings.

Close the lesson

Let children know that there will be open topic sharing during the next few days. Remind them to see you before Morning Meeting if they have serious news. Then move on to a playful activity.

Remind and reinforce in the days to follow

If a student has serious news to share, remind the class that their job is to notice how the sharer is feeling and let her know they understand. If students need a concrete reminder, keep the hand mirror handy. When students do give empathic comments, use reinforcing language: "Your words are so kind and thoughtful."

Comment and Question Starters

Empathic Sentence Starters

Guide children to notice that all the sentences have "you" in them. Teach children that the blanks should be filled in with feeling words such as "happy" and "sad." Brainstorm such words with the class.

∗ You sound _____.

∗ I'm wondering if that was _____ for you.

∗ Your expression showed that you feel _____.

∗ It looks like you are feeling _____.

∗ When you clapped, it was clear that you _____.

∗ Your face tells me that you are _____.

∗ It seems you feel _____ about that.

Question Starters

∗ **Who**   Who helped you with that?

∗ **What**   What was your favorite part about _____?

∗ **When**   When do you think you will _____?

∗ **Where**   Where were you when this happened?

∗ **Why**   Why do you think _____?

∗ **How**   How did you feel about _____?

Group Activities

**Each group activity idea in this book
takes about 2–6 minutes.**

Goals of Group Activity

* Build a class repertoire of songs, games, chants, and poems,
  which adds to a sense of community and group identity

* Encourage active and engaged participation, cooperation,
  and inclusion

* Strengthen academic and social skills

Group Activity Skills to Model

Common skills that children need for success with group
activities:

* Moving safely and staying in control of their bodies

* Speaking clearly and using an appropriate volume

* Knowing what to do when waiting for a turn

* Knowing what to do if a classmate makes a mistake

* Clapping hands on knees to keep a steady beat

Reteach common group activity skills after breaks (long weekends, vacations) and whenever new students join the class.

Scaffolding Group Activities

You can adjust the complexity of any activity to meet the class's developmental needs and abilities. For example:

* Use the Tips for Success to help prepare children for each activity. Model one element at a time. Make directions simple, clear, and consistent.

* At the beginning of the year, focus on activities that involve learning names and using simple actions and movements.

* Repeat the same activity until the class has it down before adding complexities. Young children tend to love repetition.

* As the year moves on, engage children in remembering and saying the rules of an activity: "Who can tell us the rules for this activity?"

* After doing an activity and as time allows, prompt students to reflect on what they did to be successful and what they could do next time to make it even better.

* Once children know a song or chant well, try it as a round.

* For songs, chants, and poems, start by just having children echo each line as you read it. Later, have the class say it chorally without echoing you. Still later, add movements for each line.

....

A Musical Note:

Some group activity ideas in this book involve singing. You can search online to learn the tunes or simply do these activities as chants.

Emphasize Cooperation
Over Competition

The ideas on the following pages emphasize cooperation, which helps meet Morning Meeting's goals of building community and supporting each child's sense of belonging and significance.

In activities that require individual students to come up with an answer or a creative gesture or word, emphasize helping each other out. For example, ask: "What can we do if a classmate answers incorrectly? How can we help if someone doesn't have an idea?"

If you want to introduce competition, have the group compete against itself. For example, challenge them to beat the class record in a timed game.

A Counting Rhyme

One, Two, Buckle My Shoe
—traditional

One, two, (hold up 1 finger, then 2 fingers)

Buckle my shoe; (pretend to buckle shoes)

Three, four, (hold up 3 fingers, then 4 fingers)

Shut the door; (pretend to close a door)

Five, six, (hold up 5 fingers, then 6 fingers)

Pick up sticks; (pretend to pick up sticks)

Seven, eight, (hold up 7 fingers, then 8 fingers)

Lay them straight; (pretend to lay sticks
   in a row on floor)

Nine, ten, (hold up 9 fingers, then 10 fingers)

A big fat hen! (pretend to be surprised
   to see a hen)

GROUP ACTIVITY

Skills
one-to-one
correspondence,
sequencing,
numerical order

Materials
words
displayed
(optional)

How to do it:

1 Read the rhyme to the class, pointing to each word as you read. Read it again, with the class echoing each line. Then read the entire poem as a class without the echoes.

2 Add motions like the examples listed.

3 Invite children to read or chant the rhyme in pairs or small groups.

Tip for Success

* Reinforce children's efforts to master this rhyme. For example: "You learned the words to this rhyme quickly" or "I noticed some of you using your decoding skills to figure out the trickier words."

Variations

* Use other counting rhymes, such as "The Ants Go Marching," "Five Little Apples," and "Five Little Monkeys." (You can find these online.)

* Tape picture clues over some of the words. When you get to a picture, invite a child to "read" the clue. When the child responds correctly, show and read the word, and then continue chanting.

Jolly Jump Up

How to do it:

1 Prepare a deck of 72 flash cards. For example:

* 5 shape cards (circle, square, rectangle, triangle, diamond)

* 11 number cards (0–10)

* 26 letter cards (Aa–Zz)

* 10 sight word cards (*and, book, go, he, home, look, she, stop, the, with*)

* 10 cards that say *Jolly Jump Up*

* 10 cards that say *Slowly Sit Down*

Shuffle the deck, but make sure each *Jolly Jump Up* card is followed by a *Slowly Sit Down* card.

2 Hold up each card and invite children to call out what's on it (for example, "six," "home," "triangle," and so forth).

3 When you show a *Jolly Jump Up* card, the children get up and jump until you show the *Slowly Sit Down* card. (After playing this game a few times, insert a few other movement cards throughout the deck to get the children really focusing and moving.)

Tips for Success

* Start with a smaller deck of cards (for example, just the number cards plus the *Jolly Jump Up* and *Slowly Sit Down* cards.)

* Before the activity, ask reminding questions, such as "What if somebody makes a mistake when calling out what is on the card? What could we do or say?" Then reinforce supportive behavior that you observe (for example, "I noticed people using kind words to help when someone made a mistake").

* Model safe jumping.

Bug in the Rug

How to do it:

1 Lay the "rug" on the floor in the middle of the circle.

2 Choose a child to be the scientist. She steps away from the circle and closes her eyes.

3 Silently choose a child to be the bug. He hides under the rug.

4 The scientist comes back to the circle and the rest of the children chant:

> *Bug in the rug.*
> *Bug in the rug.*
> *Who's … that …*
> *Bug in the rug?*

5 The scientist guesses who's under the rug by looking around to see who's missing. After three guesses, invite children to take turns giving clues. To limit guessing, provide a final choice between two students, one of whom is the bug.

GROUP ACTIVITY

Skills
observing, memory skills, giving clear clues

Materials
"rug" (large sheet or blanket)

6 Do a few more rounds with different students as scientists and bugs.

Tips for Success

* Model carefully crawling under the rug and emerging from under the rug. Also brainstorm with children some strategies for figuring out who the bug is when they're the scientist and for giving helpful clues if needed.

* Reinforce positive behaviors. For example: "You scientists looked around very carefully to see who was missing. There was no fooling you!"

Black Socks

How to do it:

1 Sing/chant this as a whole group, emphasizing the bold words.

> Black socks,
> they **never** get dirty.
> The longer I wear them,
> The stronger they get.
> Sometimes
> I think I should wash them
> but something inside me
> keeps saying not yet,
> not yet,
> **not yet**.

2 Pause after the last **not yet** and then repeat the song/chant.

3 Form two groups and do the song/chant as a round, with the second group coming in on the word **never**. Remember to pause after the last **not yet**.

Tip for Success

* Teach the words to the song. Remind children to pause after the last **not yet** before repeating the song/chant.

· · · · · · · · · · · · · · · · ·

Variations

* Help children create their own substitute lyrics about other items of clothing. For example: ***Knee*** socks, they ***never*** *stay up* ... or ***Shoe*** *laces, they* ***never*** *stay tied* ...

* When children are ready, try three rounds in three (or more) parts. Give each group a separate song chart to help children stay on track.

Aka Baka Soda Cracker

How to do it:

1 In a big circle, everyone does jumping jacks and chants:

> Aka baka soda cracker,
> aka baka bee.
> Aka baka soda cracker,
> one, two, three!

2 On the word *three*, everyone freezes. Those who have their feet apart sit down.

3 Restart the chant. Those sitting keep a steady beat by alternating claps and knee slaps.

4 This time, jumpers with their feet apart on *three* sit down AND sitters who end with a knee slap on *three* stand up (to join in the jumping jacks in the next round). Do several more rounds.

5 To end the game, children have to listen carefully to you. Change the last verse to:

> *Aka baka soda cracker,*
> *aka baka clown.*
> *Aka baka soda cracker,*
> *all sit down!* (everyone sits down)

Tips for Success

* Model doing safe jumping jacks and stopping and holding movements on the word *three*.

* Before the activity, ask reminding questions, such as "What could you say if you accidentally bump or kick somebody?"

* After the activity, ask a few reflective questions, such as "Were you able to predict where your feet or hands would end up?"

Lost Tooth Poem

My Tooth —anonymous

My tooth fell out and left a space
(pantomime tooth falling out)

So big my tongue can touch my face
(spread arms out wide)

And every time I smile I show
(make a big smile)

The place where something used to grow. (point to "empty" space in mouth)

I miss my tooth as you can guess
(make a sad face)

But now I have to brush one less!
(smile and pretend to brush teeth)

GROUP ACTIVITY

Skills
word recognition, reading poetry, rhyming, keeping a steady beat

Materials
poem displayed

How to do it:

1 Read the poem to the class, pointing to each word as you read. Read it again, with the class echoing each line. Then read it as a class without the echoes.

2 Brainstorm actions for each line, or use the examples above.

3 Read the poem again as a group, incorporating the actions.

Tip for Success

* Help children engage with the poem by asking questions, such as "What kinds of feelings do you have about losing a tooth?" and "Why do you think a poet might want to make us giggle about losing a tooth?"

. . . .

Variations

* Read and act out other "lost tooth" poems, such as "Wiggly Tooth" and "My Wobbly Tooth." (You can find these online.)

* Assign partners or small groups a line from the poem to read and act out.

Off My Back

How to do it:

1 Choose a student to be the guesser. Write a number on a sticky note (start with numbers between 0 and 50) and place it on the guesser's back.

2 The guesser walks around so everyone can see the number on her back and then calls on classmates to answer yes-or-no questions about the number—for example: "Is it odd or even?" "Is it greater than 25?" "Is it less than 10?"

3 When only two possible numbers are left (or whenever the guesser thinks she knows the number), the guesser says a number and takes the sticky note off to see if the guess was correct.

4 To keep the guessing from going on for too long, let the guesser ask for a "give-away" (a student whispers two numbers—the correct number and another number).

Tips for Success

* Provide a number line to help students learn how to narrow their guesses.

* Before the activity, strategize as a class some helpful questions to ask in guessing the hidden number.

* Teach children to give caring reminders when the guesser forgets a clue. Reinforce this behavior when students show it.

* *

Variation

* Instead of numbers, use names of states or countries, book titles, famous people, or other categories related to classroom learning.

Apples, Peaches, Pears, and Plums

GROUP ACTIVITY

Skills
predicting,
letter and word
recognition,
keeping a
steady beat

Materials
poem
displayed

Apples, Peaches, Pears, and Plums
—traditional

Apples, peaches, pears, and plums,
Tell me when your birthday comes!
January? February? March? April?
May? June? July? August?
September? October? November?
December?

That's when our birthdays come!

How to do it:

1 Read the poem together, keeping a steady beat. (Give two beats to each month, even those with one syllable. The stressed parts of words are in bold.)

2 Repeat the poem. This time, children stand up when their birthday month is chanted.

3 As children chant the last line, they stretch both arms up high in a cheer.

Tip for Success

* Warm students up for this activity by asking questions, such as "How many months are there in a year?" "In which month is your birthday?" "Which month do you think will have the most birthdays?"

* * * * * * * * * * * * * * * * * * *

Variation

* Change the months to seasons—*Winter?* *Spring?* *Summer?* *Fall?* Children stand when their birthday season is called.

Mouse Trap

How to do it:

1 Going around the circle, children count off, one through five.

2 Ones go outside the circle and play the role of "mice" while the others hold hands to form the "mouse trap."

3 When you say "Mouse trap, open!" the circle of children raise their hands high. The mice begin weaving in and out of the circle.

4 When you say "Mouse trap, close!" the circle of children lower their hands, trapping any mice inside the circle, where they will remain.

5 Say "Mouse trap, open!" The mice still outside the circle start weaving again.

6 Repeat until there is only one mouse left outside the circle. The round ends.

7 Play more rounds with the twos through the fives taking turns as mice.

GROUP ACTIVITY

Skills
coordination,
focusing

Materials

Tips for Success

* Before the activity, ask reminding questions, such as "What does teamwork mean? What might we do to make sure everyone has fun?"

* Decide as a class ahead of time what happens if a mouse is caught right under people's closed arms.

* After the activity, help children apply what they learned to other times of the day. For example: "During recess, what will you remember to make your games just as much fun for everyone?"

Rumpelstiltskin

An element
of surprise gets children
thinking and moving!

How to do it:

GROUP ACTIVITY

Skills
focusing,
decision-making,
deduction

Materials
chairs for
each seat
in the circle
(optional)

1 Ask for a volunteer to be the guesser. This student stands up and closes his eyes. Then silently choose someone to be "Rumpelstiltskin."

2 Remove the guesser's chair from the circle. (If on the floor, close up one seating space.)

3 The guesser, either going around the circle or randomly, asks classmates, "What's your name?" Each child responds with his or her name, except the chosen student, who responds, "Rumplestiltskin!"

4 When Rumpelstiltskin is revealed, everyone (including the guesser) quickly moves to a new seat. (Students may not move to a seat next to them.)

5 Whoever is left standing becomes the next guesser.

Tips for Success

* Model moving carefully but quickly to an available seat.

* Before the activity, briefly have children predict the benefit of asking in order around the circle versus randomly. After the activity, ask them whether their predictions (guesses) came true.

* Show enthusiasm for the children's playfulness. For example: "I heard lots of giggles—we sure had fun playing this game together" or "It was fun to see the different ways guessers asked their question."

Purple Soup

How to do it:

1 As the children sit and listen, stand and sing/chant to them.

We're making purple soup!
(hold hands together, move as if stirring)

Whip, whip ... whip, whip
(put hands on hips, wiggle right to left)

We're making purple soup!
(put hands together, move as if stirring)

Shooby dooby do
(point fingers up, twirl around)

With purple potatoes
(stretch one fist out)

And purple tomatoes
(stretch opposite fist out, place on top of other fist)

And we ...
(point thumbs at shoulders)

Want ...
(move hands away from shoulders with palms up)

YOU!
(point to another person to join in)

2 When you point to a child on *YOU!*,
that child stands and joins you in singing/
chanting. Keep pointing to someone new
on *YOU!* until the whole group is standing
and singing/chanting.

3 To end, change the last three lines to:

And we're . . .

All . . .

DONE! . . . YUM! (rub tummies)

Tips for Success

* Model the motions for each line and using an
appropriate voice volume (especially on *YOU!*).

* After some practice, invite students to substitute
a different color and other moves.

Hello, Neighbor!

Moving and singing with partners is a great way to start the day!

GROUP ACTIVITY

Skills
sequencing,
telling right
from left,
synonyms

Materials
song chart
(optional)

How to do it:

1   Students count off by twos. The ones form a circle, facing out. The twos form a larger circle around the ones, facing in. Each student should now be facing someone in the other circle, forming partnerships.

2   The class sings or chants the following. Partners do the motions toward each other.

> *Hello, neighbor! What do you say?*
> (wave, then make a questioning motion with palms up and elbows bent)

> *It's going to be a wonderful day!*
> (make wide, arching motions with arms)

> *So clap your hands and boogie on down,* (clap three times, then wiggle down)

> *Give a little bump and turn around!*
> (partners bump hips gently and turn around)

3   After the last line, the ones take a step to their right to form new partnerships.

4   Continue for several rounds.

Tips for Success

∗ Model safe and careful motions and movements in advance. You may want to teach this activity over several weeks, scaffolding it like this:

- Children stay in place in one large circle and do the motions without partners.

- In one large circle, children turn to their neighbor and do the motions.

- Children do the activity as described (or use hops or high fives in place of gentle hip bumps).

∗ Reinforce positive behaviors and academic skills. For example: "I noticed gentle hip bumps" and "What are some synonyms for 'wonderful?'"

Bluebird, Bluebird

How to do it:

1 Select one child to be the "bluebird." The class does the first verse of this song/chant while joining hands and raising them above their heads to form "windows" that the bluebird weaves in and out of.

Bluebird, bluebird, through my window.
Bluebird, bluebird, through my window.
Bluebird, bluebird, through my window.
Oh, my, I'm so tired.

2 When the class sings/chants the second verse, the bluebird chooses a second bluebird by gently tapping another child on the shoulder.

Take a student and pat her [him] on the
*   shoulder.*
Take a student and pat her [him] on the
*   shoulder.*
Take a student and pat her [him] on the
*   shoulder.*
Oh, my, I'm so tired.

3 The class goes back to the first verse while both children weave in and out of the windows. (The first bluebird walks behind the second, holding on to the second one's shoulders.) Continue adding bluebirds until all the children are bluebirds.

4 To end the song/chant, change the last line and slow down: *"Oh, bluebirds, we're so tired! ... Oh, bluebirds, sit in your nests!"*

Tip for Success

* Practice safely doing all the movements of bluebirds and windows. Encourage students to choose classmates with whom they don't usually play or work.

* *

Variation

* Replace "my" in the last line of each verse with students' names.

The Teacher's Cat

How to do it:

1 Students begin tapping out a soft, four-beat rhythm on their knees.

2 The first student starts the chant with an adjective that starts with the letter *a*. He might chant, "The **tea**cher's **cat** is an **awe**some **cat**." (Stressed beats are in bold.)

3 The next student uses an adjective that starts with *b*. For example, she might chant, "The **tea**cher's **cat** is a **beau**tiful **cat**." The third student has the letter *c* and so on around the circle.

GROUP ACTIVITY

Skills
keeping a steady beat, adjectives, alphabetical order, creative thinking

Materials
chart for adjectives

Tips for Success

* The first few times the class does this activity, brainstorm and display an alphabetical list of adjectives.

* Reinforce positive efforts. For example: "I heard some very creative words. These words will help us when we read and write."

* * * * * * * * * * * * * * * * * * * *

Variations

* Assign children letters ahead of time. Write them on index cards for children to place on the floor for reference.

* Play without following a letter order. Let children use any adjective they choose.

Who Has Seen the Wind?

Who Has Seen the Wind?
—Christina Rossetti

Who has seen the wind?
(fan on low)

Neither I nor you.

But when the leaves hang trembling,
(wiggle fingers; fan on medium)

The wind is passing through.
(sway arms side to side)

Who has seen the wind?
(fan on medium)

Neither you nor I.

But when the leaves bow down their heads,
(bend over and hang arms down; fan on high)

The wind is passing by.
(sway arms side to side)

How to do it:

1 Read the poem to the class, pointing to each word as you read. Read again, two lines at a time, with the class echoing. Then read the entire poem as a class without the echoes.

2 Choose two narrators to take turns reading, one line each. As they read, the rest of the class acts out the poem while you operate the fan to serve as the wind.

3 At the conclusion of the poem, calm the wind down by turning the fan from high to medium to low, and then off.

Tip for Success

* Before the reading, turn the fan on and off a few times and let the children enjoy the changing wind. Let them share a few observations about the fan.

Fruit Salad

This call-and-response game can support many themes and units!

How to do it:

GROUP ACTIVITY

Skills
coordination,
word and
concept
recognition

Materials
none

1 Going around the circle, children say "apple," "banana," "cherry," or "grape" in order until everyone has a fruit name.

2 Stand in the middle of the circle and call out a fruit—for example, "banana." All the children who are "bananas" quickly move to a different open spot in the circle. You should also take one of these spots.

3 One child will not get a spot. This child becomes the next caller. He or she calls out another fruit. Continue for several rounds.

4 As the game progresses, callers may call out up to three fruits at a time.

5 To end the activity, the last caller says "fruit salad!" All the children move at once to find a new seat.

Tips for Success

* Model moving safely and quickly to a new spot and what to do if two people go for the same spot. Reinforce expected behaviors.

* If children enjoy being the caller so much that they avoid finding a spot, draw children's names out of a hat.

Variation

* Instead of fruit, choose other categories that go along with something the class is studying.

Herman the Squirmin' Worm

How to do it:

1 The class sings/chants:

Sittin' on a fence post chewin' my bubble gum

Smack, smack . . . smack, smack!
(make chewing sounds)

Playin' with my yo-yo

Wooo, wooo! . . . wooo, wooo!
(pantomime playing with a yo-yo)

When along came Herman the Squirmin' Worm!
(wiggle arms)

And he was THIS BIG
(show about an inch of space between fingers)

And I said, "Herman, what happened?"

"I swallowed a leaf."

2 Repeat the song/chant, each time increasing the size of the food that Herman ate (and showing bigger and bigger sizes with hands and arms). For example:

"I swallowed a bush."

"I swallowed a tree."

"I swallowed a forest."

3 The last time through, use these words:

When along came Herman the Squirmin' Worm!

And he was THIS BIG
(show about an inch of space between fingers)

And I said, "Herman, what happened?"

"I burped!"

Tip for Success

* Before the activity, ask reminding questions, such as "How can we have fun and still keep our voices and bodies in control?" Then reinforce positive behaviors. For example: "I saw everyone being careful when they spread out their arms."

Ahoy Matey!

GROUP ACTIVITY

Skills
coordination, following directions, focusing, pantomiming

Materials
chart with list of commands (optional)

How to do it:

1 You pretend to be the Captain. Start by giving the command "ahoy matey!" Students echo this command back by standing at attention and saluting.

2 Give several other commands. Students echo each command and do the motion. Repeat "ahoy matey" between commands.

3 Once the children are familiar with all the commands, invite a student to be the Captain.

Commands

* **Ahoy matey!**—Stand at attention and salute.

* **All hands on deck!**—Walk around the "deck" (the circle).

* **Swab the deck!**—Pretend to mop the "deck."

* **Person overboard!**—Find a partner. One partner kneels while the other puts a hand on the partner's shoulder. Both pretend to search overboard with hands on foreheads.

* **Lifeboat!**—Form groups of four. Students simulate a lifeboat by placing their hands on each other's shoulders as they stand in a line.

Tips for Success

* Introduce the simpler commands before slowly teaching the more complicated ones to scaffold this activity over a few days or weeks.

* Ask reminding questions, such as "Why is it important to be a partner with other classmates sometimes?"

Super Gooney Bird

How to do it:

1 While standing in a circle, the class sings/chants:

> *Super Gooney Bird*
>
> *Had seven chicks*
>
> *Seven chicks had Super Gooney Bird*
>
> *And they couldn't fly*
>
> *And they couldn't swim*
>
> *All they did was go like this:*
>
> *Right wing!* (flap right arm)

2 Repeat the words, each time adding a new line and motion:

> *Left wing!* (flap left arm)
>
> *Right foot!* (bend right knee and move right foot forward and backward)
>
> *Left foot!* (bend left knee and move left foot forward and backward)
>
> *Chin out!* (move chin forward and backward)

GROUP ACTIVITY

Skills
coordination,
sequencing,
memory

Materials
song chart
(optional)

148

3 After a few rounds, say, "Wiggle, Waggle!"
You now become the Super Gooney Bird.
Lead the children in strutting like chickens
around the room while singing/chanting.

4 Bring the activity to a close by saying "OK,
chicks. Back to our nest!" The children return
to their seats in the circle.

Tips for Success

* Engage children in modeling safe moving. For
example: "Can someone show us a silly but safe
way that a chick might move?"

* Before adding in the singing/chanting, let children
practice doing the motions while staying in one spot
and then while following you around the room.

The Swing—
An Action Poem

The Swing
—From *A Child's Garden of Verses*
by Robert Louis Stevenson

GROUP ACTIVITY

Skills
reading with
fluency and
expression,
rhyming,
one-to-one
correspondence

Materials
poem
displayed

How do you like to go up in a swing,
Up in the air so blue?
Oh, I do think it the pleasantest thing
Ever a child can do!

Up in the air and over the wall,
Till I can see so wide,
Rivers and trees and cattle and all
Over the countryside—

Till I look down on the garden green,
Down on the roof so brown—
Up in the air I go flying again,
Up in the air and down!

How to do it:

1 Read the poem to the class, pointing to each word as you read. Read again, with the class echoing each line. Then read the entire poem as a class without the echoes.

2 Brainstorm actions for each line. For example, shrug shoulders for the first line, point and look up for the second, and so on.

3 Read the poem again as a group, incorporating the actions.

Tip for Success

* Spread this activity over a few days if needed. For example, go as far as echo reading on day one, read in unison without echoes on day two, and so forth.

Morning Messages

**Each morning message idea in this
book takes 3–7 minutes.**

Goals of Morning Message

* Build community through shared written information

* Reinforce language arts, math, and other academic skills in a
  meaningful and interactive way

* Heighten children's excitement about what they'll be learning
  that day

* Ease the transition to the rest of the day

Morning Message Skills to Model

Common skills that children need for success with morning messages:

* Looking at or reading the
  message and doing the task
  given in it before Morning
  Meeting starts

* Going up to the message
  chart to write in the date,
  circle certain words, and do
  other tasks with the message

* Knowing what to do if they
  don't understand the message
  or how to do the task

* Knowing what to do if a classmate makes a mistake in
  reading the message

* Reading the message in a
  variety of ways (see page 157
  for examples)

Reteach common morning message skills after breaks (long weekends,
vacations) and whenever new students join the class.

Scaffolding Morning Messages

You can adjust the complexity of all the messages in this book to fit students' needs and abilities. Also, keep in mind:

* Model and practice how you expect students to interact with the message as they enter the classroom before the school day starts. Some teachers also use a "Message Leader," who stands by the message as children enter. He or she helps them remember to read the message and answer the question (or start thinking about it).

* For emergent readers, repeat the same simple sentence structures and message format (see "Today, We Are Painters!" on page 158 for an example), changing only the topic of the message from day to day.

* Use picture cues to help emergent and beginning readers.

* Teach how to do a task (such as using a ruler or filling in a Venn diagram) before asking students to do it in the message.

* Begin by reading the message aloud to the class, pointing to the words as you read. Over time, move to choral reading, individual student reading, and having a student be the pointer. Introduce these elements one at a time.

* Vary the way the message is read to keep students engaged.

Morning Message Topics

Think about students' interests, needs, and abilities to determine which topics will be meaningful and engaging to them. Here's a starter list:

* Numbers (for example, students' ages, even and odd numbers, numbers children see in the room)
* Colors (clothing colors, favorite colors, and so on)
* The weather
* An activity the class will be doing that day
* Healthy foods
* Letters in students' names
* Class pet
* A plant or animal the class is observing
* Rhyming words
* Holidays
* Any content the class is studying

Morning Message Salutations

"Dear Students" is a perfectly effective salutation. But you can also mix it up some days by using salutations that are playful, match the message content, or help children become conscious of their competencies. For example:

* Dear Mathematicians,

* Greetings, Awesome Artists!

* Dear Adventurers,

* Good morning, Cooperative Students!

* Dear Team,

* Hello, Eager Readers!

* Good morning, Super Scientists!

* Dear Writers,

* Greetings, Responsible Students!

Ways to Read Morning Messages as a Class

＊ Choral read.

＊ Read in different voices (whisper, silly, loud, soft).

＊ Take turns (divide group in half; count off by twos; stand to read, sit to listen).

＊ Echo read (one or more children read a sentence, rest of class echo reads same sentence).

＊ Use "word turns" (going around circle, each person reads just one word).

＊ Silently read (call on students to paraphrase).

＊ Pantomime reading (choose words from the text, brainstorm how to use hands or bodies to pantomime the words, then read together with those actions).

＊ Chant or sing to a familiar tune.

＊ Add sound effects for the punctuation marks.

＊ Say the message salutation in another language.

＊ Include sign language for the salutation or for certain words in the body of the message.

＊ Underline adjectives and ask for synonyms.

＊ Clap the beats for words with two or more syllables.

＊ Name a reader for the day (write the child's name in a "bubble" as on page 180).

. . . .

Time Constraints

Consider any time constraints when using the "Working With the Message" steps.
For example, you may want to choose just a few of the steps to do.
Then reuse the message another day and do the other steps.

Today, We Are Painters!

Build excitement about the day ahead while practicing reading skills.

MORNING MESSAGE

Skills
recognizing letter patterns, reading left to right

Reading Level
emergent

Today is Friday.

It is sunny.

We will paint today.

Working With the Message

1 Introduce the message. For example:
"Today's message is about painting. What kinds of painting have you done?"

2 Read the message aloud as children listen. Point to each word as you read.

3 Read the message again while children point at each word from their spot.

4 Help children look ahead to their day with questions like these:

- What is fun about painting? What is tricky about painting?

- What do you think you'll paint today?

Tips for Success

* To give emergent readers needed repetition, reuse this same three-part message structure: Simply change the day, weather, and last sentence.

* Reinforce positive behaviors. For example: "I noticed lots of careful pointing. That helped keep everyone safe."

Let's Go!

MORNING MESSAGE

Skills
reading left to right and top to bottom, categorizing, counting

Reading Level
emergent

Good morning, Kindergartners!

Today is Wednesday.

How did you come to school today?

Write your name on a sticky note. Put it under the right word and picture.

Bus   Car   Walk   Bike

Mrs. Roser

Working With the Message

1 Before you read the message, ask, "Where should my pointer be as I begin to read? Is this the top of the page or the bottom? The left or the right?" As you read, point at each word.

2 Choral count the sticky notes in each column. Ask, "Which picture on our message has the most names below it? Which has the least?"

3 As time allows, extend the discussion:

- Can you think of other ways a student might get to school?

- If you had to travel a long, long way, would you walk? Why or why not?

Tip for Success

* If needed, write names on sticky notes for children to post.

. . . .

Variation

* Adapt the message for other things students can categorize and count, such as colors and shapes.

What Color Are You Wearing?

MORNING MESSAGE

Skills
pre-reading strategies,
color recognition,
self-awareness,
most and least

Reading Level
emergent

Dear Friends,

Today is Monday.

It is sunny and windy outside.

Put a check mark next to **one** color that you are wearing.

Black	Orange
Blue	Pink
Brown	Purple
Gray	Red
Green	Yellow

Working With the Message

1 Read the message to the class. Choral read a second time.

2 Ask a few reflective questions, such as "Why did you pick that one color?"

3 Have students who checked the same color read aloud a line of the message together.

4 Before counting check marks, ask, "Does anyone have a guess about which color we checked the most? The least?"

5 Count the check marks chorally. Again ask which color has the most checks and which the least. To extend learning, make a bar graph if time allows.

Tip for Success

* Reinforce academic skills and positive behaviors. For example: "Your careful counting helped us figure out which color we checked the most and which one we checked the least."

Wild Weather!

MORNING MESSAGE

Skills
summarizing, recall, most and least

Reading Level
emergent

Dear Chilly Children,

Today is Wednesday, January 11, 2012.

 It is snowy outside.

It is very cold. Brrrrrr!

 Thinking Questions:

What do you do to keep warm in the winter?

What things do you use to keep warm?

Be ready to share.

Working With the Message

1 Say to children, "We'll be reading the message chorally in a 'shivery' way." Ask questions such as these:

- What might our voices sound like if we were very cold? What could we do with our bodies to show this?

2 Choral read using the voices and motions children suggest.

3 As time allows, record a few volunteers' warming strategies. If another child shares the same strategy, put a check mark next to it.

4 Discuss the message with questions like these:

- Which warming idea has the most check marks? The least? Who can find the capital letters on our chart? What two letters make a "ch" sound?

Tip for Success

* Reinforce academic skills and positive behaviors. For example: "What a lot of creative shivery sounds!"

· ·

Variation

* Use this message structure before any exciting event. For example, a thinking question could be "How do you stay safe on a field trip?"

Let's Exercise!

MORNING MESSAGE

Skills
writing, drawing, exercising for good health

Reading Level
emergent

Dear Excited Exercisers,

Today is Friday. It is June 1, 2012.

Today is our Field Day—HOORAY!

Draw a picture or write a word to show what you like to do outside:

RUN

basbl

Working With the Message

1 Read the message aloud. Then choral read the message in a whisper (since students may be excited).

2 Point to a drawing or word that a student supplied. Invite individual children to say their word or briefly explain their picture. Repeat as time allows.

3 Focus on the exercise theme. For example, ask:

- Why do you think exercise is good for your health? What is one thing that a lot of you like to do for exercise? Are there any activities you would like to learn more about?

Tip for Success

* Reinforce the importance of exercise. For example: "I see many different ways to exercise—you have given me some new ideas on how I can stay healthy!"

Variation

* Adapt the message to help children plan their learning. For example: "Draw a picture or write a word to show what you would like to do at choice time today."

An Apple a Day

After using a three-part message structure (page 158), try this slightly more challenging one.

MORNING MESSAGE

Skills
nutritional aware-
ness, spelling,
patience

Reading Level
emergent

Today is Tuesday.

It is cloudy.

Healthy foods help us stay healthy!

Guess what healthy food I like.

<u>a</u> <u>p</u> _ _ _

Draw a healthy food you like.

Working With the Message

1 Introduce the message: "We're going to guess a mystery word in our message today. But wait for my signal before you say your guess. What could help you wait quietly?"

2 Point to each word as you read. Read again, inviting children to point at each word from their spot.

3 Make the "ap" sound of the mystery word. Tell children to stand and keep silent when they're ready to guess. Then say: "I'll count to three. Then we'll say our guess together: One, two, three— APPLE!"

4 Have children study the pictures they drew. Ask questions like these:

  • What do you notice about our healthy foods? What do you think makes a food healthy? What does your favorite healthy food taste like? Is it sweet? Spicy? What other words can we use to talk about food?

Tip for Success

* Reinforce positive behaviors. For example: "You all showed self-control and patience as you waited for your classmates to be ready to guess."

How Many Buttons?

MORNING MESSAGE

Skills
one-to-one correspondence, addition

Reading Level
beginning

Dear Careful Counters,

Today is Wednesday.

It is sunny and breezy outside.

Count the buttons you have on. Then draw the buttons in a box below. Write your name in the box. If you do not have buttons, write only your name.

Mrs. Roser ⊡⊡⊡				Lydia
		Freddie ⊡⊡		
	Helen			

Working With the Message

1 Read the message. Then ask, "What was it like to count your buttons? If counting was hard, how could you make it easier?"

2 Read the message again. Point to each word as you read.

3 Chorally count the buttons in each box. Write the number in each box.

4 As time allows, extend learning with questions like these:

- Can anyone add up their number of buttons with a classmate's number of buttons? What would that sound (or look) like in "math language" (for example, 3 + 2 = 5 or 3 + 0 = 3)?

- How many buttons do you think are in our class today? How could we find out?

Tip for Success

* Reinforce math thinking. For example: "You are thinking like mathematicians."

Music Makers

MORNING MESSAGE

Skills
categorizing,
punctuation,
music

Reading Level
beginning

Today is Thursday.

Sarah is first today.

We will continue to rehearse for our music performance with Mrs. Bernal.

 What kinds of music have you heard? What instruments can you name? Be ready to share.

Working With the Message

1 Ask a student to circle the periods and another to circle the question marks.

2 Choral read the message, using the punctuation sounds (see Tip for Success).

3 After reading the message, draw two columns below the questions: *Kinds of Music* and *Instruments*. As children share ideas, list them.

4 Briefly discuss the message, prompting with questions like these:

- Do you know of any other punctuation marks that are not in our message? What might they sound like? How can music help us in our lives?

Tip for Success

* Before reading the message, brainstorm ideas for sound effects to go with the punctuation marks (such as a *ding* for periods and *hmm* for question marks). Tell children that as they read the message, they're going to make those punctuation sounds with their voices.

Variation

* Invite a volunteer to be the maestro, leading the "punctuation orchestra" as the class choral reads the message.

What's Your Name?

MORNING MESSAGE

Skills
finding patterns, making comparisons, using alphabetical order

Reading Level
beginning

Dear Friends,

Today is Wednesday.

This is our second week of school.

We will play more name games today.

Look at our class list below and see what you notice.

Ahmed	Jorani	Rachel
Aliya	Kenny	Robby
Ben	Kristen	Rosa
Dao-ming	Layla	Sammy
Emilio	Marco	Tomas
Gretchen	Misha	Tyler
Jin-ping	Morgan	Zeneb

Working With the Message

1 List names in alphabetical order.

2 During the meeting, invite students to read aloud each line of the message.

3 Focus students' attention on the names. For example: "What do you notice about our names? If you don't know how to read a name, what could you do?"

4 Invite a few volunteers to read their name or a classmate's name (if a classmate's name, you choose it).

Tip for Success

* Reinforce positive behaviors. For example: "I saw quiet and still bodies, eyes on the chart, and patience for classmates."

. . . .

Variations

* Use sticky notes and reorganize names as a class (for example, by short or long names).

* Dismiss children from Morning Meeting in alphabetical (or reverse alphabetical) order.

Time to Rhyme!

Thursday, April 12, 2012

Dear Readers and Rhymers,

Today's a new day
For work and for play.

Can you rhyme more than Sam
In *Green Eggs and Ham*?

Here, write some rhymes
And we'll have some good times!

Bell	Day	Hat
well	say	CAT
TELL	pay	pat
	MAY	sat

Working With the Message

1 Before reading the message, ask what students notice about it (focus on rhyming words). Then invite them to count off by threes and form three groups. Read the salutation.

2 Have ones read aloud the first stanza, twos the second, and threes the third.

3 Ask a student from each group to identify which words in their stanza rhyme and circle those words on the chart.

4 Have each group read one column of the rhyming words students wrote. Brainstorm more words to list. If time allows, ask questions like these:

• What authors use rhymes? What favorite songs have rhymes? What could we do with our rhyming words?

Tip for Success

* Review and reinforce skills for reading aloud in groups. For example: "What should we do with our voices when we read together?" and "You read rhythmically together. I heard the beats in your voices."

How Does Your Garden Grow?

Today is Tuesday, May 15, 2012.

It is cloudy.

Our bean plants are growing by leaps and bounds!

How many inches tall do you think your plant is today? Write the number below. Then use a ruler to check.

10

4

9

7

Working With the Message

1 Choral read the message. Then ask, "What do you think I mean by 'leaps and bounds'?"

2 Invite children to imitate growing plants with their bodies. Take several ideas.

3 Focus on the height estimates that children wrote with questions like these:

- What strategies did you use to help you estimate? Some of you thought your plant would be very tall today. Why? Who remembers what things help plants grow?

Tips for Success

* Have a few class plants for children to care for (potato plants do well indoors). Since plants can sprawl, have children track just one stem's growth. Also have some rulers on hand for measuring.

* Practice, review, and reinforce measuring skills. For example: "I see careful handling of our rulers" and "Lots of people looked at their last measurements before making a guess. That's thinking like a scientist!"

Guest Teacher

MORNING MESSAGE

Skills
responsibility,
empathy

Reading Level
beginning

Message reader: Olivia

Today is Thursday, November 10, 2011.

Dear Students,

Today, I am at a teachers' meeting. We have a guest teacher. Her name is Ms. Johnson.

You can work together to make today a great day!

 Thinking Question

How will you follow our class rules today? Be ready to share.

Working With the Message

1 Before the student reader reads the message, the guest teacher asks, "While Olivia reads the message, what will you do to follow the Morning Meeting rules? How else can we help each other today?"

2 After the student reader reads the message, the guest teacher invites the children to share their ideas for following the rules. Prompting questions might include:

- How can you help each other get back on track if you forget a rule? How can I help you?
- What might be challenging without your regular teacher? What might be interesting?

Tip for Success

* The day before, select a student to read the message and practice together. Also, remind children of the importance of following the rules when they have a guest teacher. For example: "When might it be especially hard to follow the rules?"

Variation

* Adapt the message for guest speakers and other classroom visitors.

My Name Starts With...

MORNING MESSAGE

Skills
letter recognition and formation, making predictions, graphing

Reading Level
beginning

Today is Tuesday, November 15, 2011. It is sunny.

Good morning, Graph Makers!

We have had lots of fun making graphs together.

Today, we will make a bar graph with the first letters of our first names.

Write the first letter of your first name on a sticky note. Place the sticky note on our graph.

A B C D E F G H I J K L M N O P Q R S T U V W X Y Z

Working With the Message

1 Before Morning Meeting (as children enter the classroom), help them place their sticky notes. Guide them in making predictions. For example: "Do you think our names use every letter in the alphabet?" and "Which letter do you predict will have the highest bar?"

2 During Morning Meeting, read aloud one line at a time and have students echo you.

3 Invite children to lead the pointing and choral counting of the sticky notes in each column.

4 Guide students in analyzing the graph with questions like these:

- Who can make a true math statement about our graph? What title might we give our graph, and why?

Tips for Success

* As an example, place your own initial on the graph before children arrive.

* Reinforce academic skills and positive behaviors. For example: "You adjusted your sticky notes so they went up in a straight line. I see very neat letter writing."

Favorite Numbers

Use children's favorite numbers to engage them with math.

MORNING MESSAGE

Skills
sequencing,
computation skills

Reading Level
fluent

¡Hola, Niños!

Today is Wednesday, January 4, 2012.

Garth is first today. Blanca is the door holder.

Today, we will do lots of work with numbers. Write a number you like on a sticky note. Then post it here:

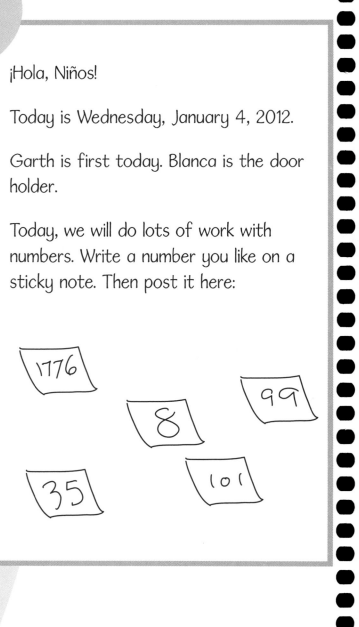

Working With the Message

1 Choral read the salutation.

2 Ask for volunteers to read each sentence of the message.

3 Work with students' sticky notes. For example:

- Rearrange numbers from smallest to largest as a child calls out what number should come next. Then ask, "What strategies did you use to put these numbers in order?"

- Ask students for other mathematical ways to order the sticky notes (largest to smallest, numbers that add up to 50 or 100, and so on).

- Direct students to look at their own number. Then ask, "If you added the digits together, do you think the sum would be less than 10 or more than 10? Why?"

Tip for Success

* Reinforce children's enthusiasm for math. For example: "We're really thinking like mathematicians. What fun numbers can be!"

Variation

* Adapt the message for social studies. For example: "Today, we will learn about the world of work. Write a job you want to study on a sticky note. Post it here."

How's the Weather?

MORNING MESSAGE

Skills
weather vocabulary, letter-sound recognition

Reading Level
fluent

Today is Monday, October 24, 2011. It is raining.

Dear Meteorologists,

Today, we will make weather sounds.

How many weather words can you remember? Write a weather word here:

Windy   lightning

hot

cool   tHunder   HAiL

muggy

rain

Working With the Message

1 Introduce "weather sounds." Ask, "What weather sounds have you heard?"

2 Brainstorm ways to make a sound for most of the words listed (for example, *whoosh* for *windy*).

3 Point to or read a word (*windy*). Have everyone make the sound associated with it (*whoosh*). Repeat for a few words.

4 Now read a word and invite just one student to make the sound. Repeat for a few words.

Tip for Success

* Reinforce academic skills and positive behaviors. For example: "You all controlled your voices so that our volume was just right." "A few weeks ago, you knew just a few weather words. Now you know so many!"

. . . .

Variations

* Point to each weather word the children wrote. Invite the child who wrote the word to say it aloud.

* Introduce weather-related concepts. For example: "Who knows what a weather forecast is?"

Today Is a Special Day

This message works for any special day or month.

Tuesday, January 17, 2012

Dear Students,

Yesterday was a holiday for Martin Luther King, Jr. He wanted to make life in our country fair for all. That was his dream.

Martin Luther King, Jr., was a brave person and a hero. Later, we will read a book about him.

Do you have a dream for our country? Write or draw it here:

Working With the Message

1 Read the message to the class.

2 Explain how you gathered information about Dr. King (from the Internet, books, and so on).

3 Discuss the message and responses with the class. For example:

- What do you think makes a person a hero? Who has ideas about why Dr. King was a hero?

- Who are your heroes? Where can we learn more about our heroes?

- What's the difference between having a dream for yourself and having a dream for your country?

Tip for Success

* Before working with the message, display the sources you used to learn about the holiday. Explain that we can better appreciate holidays, people, historical events, and so on when we learn more about them and share what we learn.

Count Your Name

Tuesday, September 27, 2011

Dear Mathematicians,

Today, we will talk about odd and even numbers. Can you think of things that come in odd numbers and things that come in even numbers? Hmm . . .

Count how many letters are in your first name. Is the number odd or even? Write your name under Odd or Even below.

ODD NUMBER	EVEN NUMBER
Kim	Jessie
Grayson	Kwon

Working With the Message

1 To help children tap prior knowledge, ask, "Our message today is about odd and even numbers. What do you already know about odd and even numbers?"

2 Invite children to form two groups: "Those with an odd number of letters in their name, sit on this side of the circle; those with an even number of letters, sit on the other side."

3 Have groups take turns reading sentences. Then ask questions like these:

- What do you notice about the number of letters in our names? Do more names have an odd number or an even number of letters? What are some other things that are odd or even?

Tip for Success

* Reinforce positive behaviors. For example: "What great ideas you came up with for odd and even things in our world!" And for a quick extension, invite children to count using only odd or only even numbers.

Variation
* Adapt the message for practicing categorizing skills in science.

Where in the World?

MORNING MESSAGE

Skills
categorizing,
geography

Reading Level
fluent

Wednesday, February 8, 2012
It is cold and cloudy outside.

Welcome aboard, Travelers!

Let's continue our journey around the world!

Write one place we have learned about or one place you want to visit. Use **red** for a **city**, **blue** for a **state**, **green** for a **country**, and **orange** for a **continent**.

NYC   Texas   Mexico
Vietnam   Africa

Bon voyage!
Your Captain,
Mrs. Roser

Working With the Message

1 Invite a student to read the message. Before she begins, remind listeners: "What will our job as the audience be while Sonya reads the message to us?"

2 Invite another student to pick a category (or a color). The class then choral reads the words in that category as the student points to them. Continue with another category until all words are read.

3 Extend learning with questions like these:
- Who can show us where the place they wrote is on our world map? How long do you think it might take to fly to Mexico City? Africa?

Tip for Success

* Before reading the message, point out any tricky words the class may need help with. Reinforce academic success. For example: "This unit seemed hard when we started, but look at how much we've learned! That shows perseverance."

Variations

* Adapt the message for language arts: Use parts of speech or book genres.

* Adapt the message for science: Use categories such as animal habitats.

How Do We Do It?

Tuesday, April 10, 2012

MORNING MESSAGE

Skills
verbs and adverbs, creative writing, brainstorming

Reading Level
fluent

Dear Storytellers,

Yesterday, we joyfully read a poem together. Today, we'll write creatively together.

Storytellers skillfully use words to describe the actions people do. These words help make a story come to life. Write an action that people do and how they do it.

Actions	How We Can Do These Actions
walk	slowly
sing	softly

Working With the Message

1 Choral read as a whole group.

2 Choose two or three actions. Ask children how they might safely show each action while sitting. (Example: Use two fingers to show "walking quickly.")

3 Choral read the message and the selected actions, adding motions.

4 Ask about the words students added to the message. For example:

- What do you notice about many of the words in our "How We Can Do These Actions" list? (If children don't notice the *ly*, point it out to them.) How do words like these make our writing more interesting to readers?

Tips for Success

* Before reading the message together, help students with challenging words. For example: "Today's message has some big words. Can anyone define *joyfully? Creatively? Skillfully?*"

* Reinforce children's creativity. For example: "You came up with some very descriptive words to show how people do things."

Searching the Solar System

MORNING MESSAGE

Skills
organization, classification, compare and contrast

Reading Level
fluent

Friday, May 11, 2012

Dear Planet Experts,

Yesterday, you worked hard on your planet research projects. Today, we will gather more facts to share with our planet partners.

At our Morning Meeting, we will work together to place planets in the Venn diagram below.

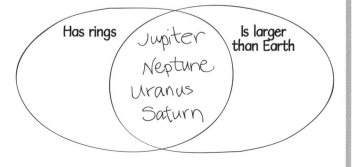

Working With the Message

1 Choral read the message together.

2 Pair children up. Assign each pair a planet and tell them to discuss where it goes on the Venn diagram. (More than one pair can have the same planet.)

3 Call on pairs to share their ideas. Invite volunteers to complete the diagram.

4 Discuss the finished diagram. For example: "Our Venn diagram gives us lots of information! Do you see anything that surprises you?"

Tip for Success

* Before using this message, review what children know about Venn diagrams. For example: "We've used Venn diagrams before. What do you remember about how to use them?"

Variations

* Adapt the content: For social studies, use countries or historic figures.

* Adapt the message: For younger students, place two intersecting Hula-hoops on the floor and sort with objects instead of using a Venn diagram.

Sample Combinations

of Greeting, Sharing, Group Activity, and
Morning Message Ideas

When planning a Morning Meeting, consider your goals for students, their developmental needs and abilities, and how much time you have. Remember, you know your students best, so combine and adapt ideas in ways that work best for them.

Here are a few sample combinations:

Beginning of the Year

When students are adjusting to a new teacher, new classmates, and a new grade, these simple ideas invite everyone to participate in a comfortable way.

Greeting:	Here We Are Together (p. 40)
Sharing:	Apples or Bananas? (p. 64)
Group Activity:	A Counting Rhyme (p. 112)
Morning Message:	Today, We Are Painters! (p. 158)

Reinforcing Specific Skills

You can put together a greeting, sharing, group activity, and morning message combination to reinforce skills the class is working on. For example, these ideas help strengthen skills in math while incorporating social skills, such as speaking in front of a group and making connections.

Greeting:	Skip Two (p. 36)
Sharing:	Reporting Food Finds (p. 84)
Group Activity:	Off My Back (p. 124)
Morning Message:	How Many Buttons? (p. 170)

Reinforcing Content Themes

You can also focus a Morning Meeting on a particular content area. Here are two combinations that reinforce a science theme.

Greeting:	Magnifying Glass (p. 50)
Sharing:	Asking Questions (p. 98)
Group Activity:	Bug in the Rug (p. 116) or Herman the Squirmin' Worm (p. 144)
Morning Message:	How Does Your Garden Grow? (p. 178)

Greeting:	Magnifying Glass (p. 50)
Sharing:	My Favorite Season . . . (p. 68)
Group Activity:	Bluebird, Bluebird (p. 136)
Morning Message:	How's the Weather? (p. 186)

Before Special Events

When an exciting event is planned for the day, you can use a combination like this to provide children with an outlet for their energy while helping them maintain self-control. This combination can also be used on low-energy days to provide a needed spark for the learning ahead.

Greeting:	Round the Circle (p. 42)
Sharing:	Questions & Comments (p. 102)
Group Activity:	Mouse Trap (p. 128)
Morning Message:	Let's Exercise! (p. 166) or
	Music Makers (p. 172)

Time Considerations

If you select an idea that might take the class somewhat longer to do (for example, when you need to do some modeling first), choose simpler and shorter ideas for the other components of the meeting. You can also adapt ideas to meet time constraints (for example, by cutting out a step or two or by simplifying a step).

Daily Morning Meeting Planner

Date: _____ Today's special events: _____

Curriculum connections: _____

	Skills to focus on/reinforce	Notes/reflections
Greeting		
Sharing *Format (circle one):* Around-the-Circle, Partner, Dialogue		
Group Activity *Type (circle one):* Song, Chant, Poem, Game, Other		
Morning Message Topic: How to read/work with the message:		

Weekly Morning Meeting Planner

Date: _____ This week's special events: _____

Curriculum connections: _____

Skills to focus on or reinforce: _____

	Monday	Tuesday	Wednesday	Thursday	Friday
Greeting					
Sharing					
Group Activity					
Morning Message					

Reflections:

Teacher Language

That Enriches Morning Meeting

Reinforcing Language

When you observe positive behaviors during Morning Meeting, remember to use reinforcing language to reflect back what students are doing well. Here are some examples:

* We are getting good at keeping control of our bodies.

* You showed that we can work together as a team.

* You took care of each other when someone made a mistake. What a caring class we have!

* You waited patiently for your turn to talk.

* I saw lots of careful listening. You had your eyes on the speaker and your bodies were quiet and still.

* I heard everyone singing [speaking, chanting, etc.] in a clear voice.

* You followed directions very well. You moved quickly but patiently, just like we practiced.

* You are giving many specific details to support your ideas.

* You are counting the check marks carefully.

* You are thinking like real mathematicians [scientists, artists, etc.].

To learn more about reinforcing language, read *The Power of Our Words: Teacher Language That Helps Children Learn*, 2nd ed., by Paula Denton, EdD (Center for Responsive Schools, 2014), available at www.responsiveclassroom.org.

Open-Ended Questions

Use questions such as the following to elicit more than a "yes" or "no"—for example, to prompt positive behaviors before doing an activity and to prompt reflective thinking afterward:

* What will we need to do to make this successful?

* Which of our class rules might be hard for us during this [activity]?

* What could we do to support one another?

* What happens if someone makes a mistake? What words might we say?

* What made that work? What made it fun?

* What strategies did you use?

* What was challenging about that?

* What was a way we followed our rules?

* How might this help us later during math? Reading? Recess?

Morning Meeting Resources

All the ideas in this book come from or are consistent with the *Responsive Classroom*® approach to teaching, in which Morning Meeting is a key practice. To learn more, see the following resources published by Center for Responsive Schools and available from www.responsiveclassroom.org.

The Morning Meeting Book, 3rd ed., by Roxann Kriete and Carol Davis. 2014.

80 Morning Meeting Ideas for Grades 3–6, by Carol Davis. 2012.

99 Activities and Greetings: Great for Morning Meeting … and Other Meetings, Too! by Melissa Correa-Connolly. 2004.

Doing Math in Morning Meeting: 150 Quick Activities That Connect to Your Curriculum by Andy Dousis and Margaret Berry Wilson. 2010.

Doing Science in Morning Meeting: 150 Quick Activities That Connect to Your Curriculum by Lara Webb and Margaret Berry Wilson. 2013.

Doing Language Arts in Morning Meeting: 150 Quick Activities That Connect to Your Curriculum by Jodie Luongo, Joan Riordan, and Kate Umstatter. 2015.

Doing Social Studies in Morning Meeting: 150 Quick Activities That Connect to Your Curriculum by Leah Carson and Jane Cofie. 2017.

For articles about Morning Meeting, and to learn more about Interactive Modeling (a powerful teaching practice that helps children learn routines and skills, including those needed for Morning Meeting), visit www.responsiveclassroom.org.

To see video clips of Morning Meeting in action in real classrooms, visit youtube.com/user/responsiveclassroom.

The Responsive Classroom® Approach

Morning Meeting is just one practice of the widely used, evidence-based *Responsive Classroom* approach to teaching. The *Responsive Classroom* approach is associated with increases in academic achievement, decreases in problem behaviors, improvements in social skills, and higher-quality instruction. To learn more, visit www.responsiveclassroom.org.

Acknowledgments

Many of the ideas I offer in this book came out of my classroom experiences and the work I've done since then with children and teachers around the country. A big hug and my lasting thanks go to those eager young children and their dedicated teachers.

Writing a book is always a journey of highs, lows, confusion, and epiphany, and being able to take that journey together with one of your best friends provides a life memory that will always be cherished. Carol Davis, professional development designer with Northeast Foundation for Children (NEFC), was with me every step of the journey. Her guidance and support were invaluable in bringing this book from idea to completion. I'd also like to thank my colleague, Jim Brissette, project manager and editor of this book. Jim became our journey's fearless "field guide." He knows all of the many rough roads, shortcuts, and scenic vistas, and was always quick to help us stay on track with a laugh and a smile. [Publisher's note: Northeast Foundation for Children is the former name of Center for Responsive Schools.]

And, if this book was a journey, Marlynn Clayton, co-founder of NEFC, was certainly the one who originally drew the map. Marlynn's ability to translate good ideas into actual practice has influenced more than one generation of teachers and their students. Thank you, Marlynn.

For their keen insights in reviewing the manuscript, my appreciation goes to elementary school teachers Kirsten Howard and Jean O'Quinn. I greatly appreciate the many contributions made to the publication of this book by the wonderful professionals at NEFC, especially Roxann Kriete, Karen Casto, Mary Beth Forton, Richard Henning, Helen Merena, Cathy Hess, Elizabeth Nash, and Alice Yang.

Finally, I'd like to thank my gifted husband, Mark, and our creative sons, Will and Wes, for their patience and encouragement. Their love, support, and laughter are always with me on whatever road I choose to travel.

ABOUT THE PUBLISHER

Center for Responsive Schools, Inc., a not-for-profit educational organization, is the developer of *Responsive Classroom®*, an evidence-based education approach associated with greater teacher effectiveness, higher student achievement, and improved school climate. *Responsive Classroom* practices help educators build competencies in four interrelated domains: engaging academics, positive community, effective management, and developmentally responsive teaching. We offer the following resources for educators:

Professional Development Services

* Workshops for K–8 educators (locations around the country and internationally)

* On-site consulting services to support implementation

* Resources for site-based study

* Annual conferences for K–8 educators

Publications and Resources

* Books on a wide variety of *Responsive Classroom* topics

* Free monthly newsletter

* Extensive library of free articles on our website

For details, contact:

Responsive Classroom®

Center for Responsive Schools, Inc.
85 Avenue A, P.O. Box 718
Turners Falls, Massachusetts 01376-0718

800-360-6332   www.responsiveclassroom.org
info@responsiveclassroom.org